GIRLFRIEND

RANDOM HOUSE

NEW YORK

MEN,
WOMEN,
AND
DRAG

TEXT BY
HOLLY BRUBACH

PHOTOGRAPHS BY
MICHAEL JAMES
O'BRIEN

Library of Congress Cataloging-in-Publication Data

Brubach, Holly.
Girlfriend: men, women, and drag/Holly Brubach;
with photographs by Michael James O'Brien.
p. cm.
ISBN 0-679-41443-6
1. Transvestism.   2. Female impersonators.   3. Male impersonators.
I. Title.
HQ77.B7   1999   306.77—dc21   98-35604

Printed in the United States of America on acid-free paper
Random House website address: www.atrandom.com
24689753
First Edition

Book design by J. K. Lambert

There is only one sex left; we are all women in spirit.

MONTESQUIEU

CONTENTS

AGITATION

The difference between the sexes is, happily, one of great profundity. Clothes are but the symbol of something hid deep beneath.

VIRGINIA WOOLF,
Orlando

....

Before drag sent out the tremors that have been shaking the foundations of our culture for the past few years, there were rumblings in the fashion world, which is my neighborhood. The signals that the ground was about to shift beneath our feet went beyond the occasional drag queen shuffled in among the supermodels—a favorite stunt of designers like Thierry Mugler and Todd Oldham. The androgyny of the seventies—when homosexuals and lesbians declared themselves the conscientious objectors in the war between the sexes, and men and women attempted to overcome the vast distance between them by meeting in the middle—had clearly failed, and the goal of a unisex Utopia, in which everyone would wear blue jeans and jumpsuits, had been dismissed as impracticable, to say nothing of dull. In its place, something subtle and far-reaching was emerging. A new, more playful exchange, with men and women insisting on their differences but raiding each other's wardrobes, had been gathering momentum since the early eighties; by the time the nineties dawned, it proved impossible to ignore.

In retrospect, the early indications appeared in the ordinarily placid realm of menswear. A spontaneous debate had sprung up around the suit. Rei Kawakubo, in her Comme des Garçons collection, proposed a ruffle at the back of the jacket, or a new three-piece ver-

sion—a jacket and a skirt worn over trousers. Jean Paul Gaultier introduced a pin-striped vest (worn with trousers, a shirt, and tie) cut,
like a woman's ballgown, with an off-the-shoulder neckline and
draped into a bustle and a sweeping train. John Bartlett outfitted men
in suits with high-heeled pumps and dark red lipstick painted in the
pinched shape of a Kewpie-doll mouth. This was, if memory serves,
around the time that "suit" became synonymous with a man who is
stuffy, smug, humorless, and clueless, a paragon of cookie-cutter
masculinity—as in, "The funny new ad campaign was vetoed by the
suits."

And then there were the designers for women, who all the while
continued to borrow styles that had initially belonged to men, as if the
men's rights to them had expired and the styles had now passed into
the public domain. Even boxer shorts had been adapted for women.
Just when it began to seem that there was nothing left to appropriate,
Vivienne Westwood presented a flesh-colored bodysuit with an erect
penis and testicles drawn on the groin or, on another occasion, shoes
with miniature penises projecting upward from the toes.

As a journalist whose job it was to cover fashion's progress, I looked
on as these developments were consistently eclipsed by clothes regarded as "wearable"; even Westwood's penis-as-fashion-accessory—
a wake-up call if ever there was one—went largely unremarked,
which is perhaps hardly surprising. New ideas, ones that pose a threat
to the status quo, often turn up first in fashion, where it's safe to say
just about anything, if only because fashion is considered frivolous
and inconsequential. A fashion show may be dismissed as mere entertainment, but in the end its entertainment value makes the audience
more disposed to its subliminal messages. Charles Ludlam, the play-
wright, actor, and founder of the Ridiculous Theatrical Company,
who often worked in drag and wrote drag roles, maintained that "if
you're going to tell people the truth, you have to make them laugh or
they'll kill you."

It was during those years that the postmodern era in fashion got
under way, and those of us who were watching it unfold soon realized
that, as in other fields, its hallmark would be pastiche. Inspired by the
century's debris that had piled up in thrift shops, designers took to
lifting elements from disparate sources and combining them. Prior
decades, far-flung cultures—everything was fair game: a military

jacket was paired with a sarong skirt and worn with 1940s platform shoes. Stock characters like the ranch hand, the stripper, the lumberjack, the nerd, the nurse, the secret agent, and the biker were dismantled, then reassembled with the references scrambled. Celebrities like Audrey Hepburn and Marilyn Monroe came in for cannibalization. Creative control passed from the designers, who invent the clothes, to the stylists, who put them together. In short, fashion had begun to do what drag had always done: explicitly referring to its sources, commenting on them, adopting an ironic stance. Designers and drag queens suddenly found themselves engaged in the same operation. The ruffles and the bustle attached to a man's suit constituted a partial, or modular, form of drag. What had started out quirky and small, off in a corner, soon grew to such vigorous proportions that fashion could no longer contain it.

....

Though drag is by no means a recent invention (Caesar's nephew, Louis XIV's brother, Benvenuto Cellini, Samuel Pepys all did it), its current heyday is unprecedented in America: at no time in our history have so many people taken up the clothing of the opposite sex, and in such an exuberant, public manner. At first glance, this may appear to be nothing more than a raucous, end-of-the-millennium costume party that got off to an early start. And there is that aspect to it, though the revelry seems born not so much of celebration as of frustration and the need to blow off steam in the face of sex roles that are too constricting. But with the benefit of a closer look, we recognize that drag's recent emergence is not so spur-of-the-moment, that it is in fact the culmination of a process that has been going on for decades.

The groundwork was laid by feminism and gay liberation, which together ushered in a climate of anarchy, freedom, and confusion. The culture of exhibitionism, for which the club scene of the early eighties served as an incubator, and the fitness craze have legitimized people's urge to make a spectacle of themselves and rewarded it with the applause of a willing audience. An escalating preoccupation with status and fashion has heightened our awareness of clothes and the information they encode. A premium on celebrity has elevated the famous people who appear in magazines and movies to the status of icons, to such an extent that they no longer own their own faces. Together, these developments have conspired to make drag compelling and timely. In recent years, it has been enriched and its numbers swollen by an influx of newcomers who view it as a vehicle for themselves and for their ideas. In its present incarnation, drag is the medium in which art, performance, and fashion converge.

It is a loaded topic, as I learned early on, triggering ferocious responses in a wide variety of people—even, or perhaps especially, in those people who know little or nothing about it. In general, the opposition subdivides into several camps, each of which reviles drag for its own reasons. There are men (both straight and gay) who abhor drag for its flamboyant display and find it alarming that the transition from masculine to feminine can be made by means of something so facile as a change of clothes, that a man's lifelong cultivation of the masculine virtues can fall away so quickly, that femininity resides so close to home. There are men (straight and gay) fascinated with the transformation—some who wouldn't go near a drag bar but who want to know everything that goes on inside, and others who are seasoned spectators, who go out and look at drag queens the way some guys watch *Monday Night Football*. There are men who deeply resent drag: "I despise drag queens," one married man, an incorrigible flirt, told me, "for trashing everything that I hold dear."

As for women, there are those who consider drag queens their soul sisters, and others who feel insulted by drag as a mean-spirited, sexist caricature, a send-up that misrepresents them and pokes fun at them. There are women irate because they feel that drag queens have appropriated many of the tactics that for centuries have constituted their powers of attraction and, having exposed those tactics for what they are—time-honored devices rather than innate characteristics—have dispelled any mystery that once surrounded them, rendering them ineffectual.

There are intellectuals (men and women alike) who champion drag as a laboratory for what is known in academic circles as "gender studies," where hypotheses about the masculine and the feminine are put into practice and tested. There are the puritans, who mistakenly assume that drag is about kinky sex rather than about conventional sex roles. There are the jaded, who dismiss drag as nothing more than a passing fad, like a trend in hemlines—devoid of ideas. "It's so *over*,"

PLATE 1

PLATE 2

PLATE 3

PLATE 4

PLATE 5

PLATE 6

PLATE 7

PLATE 8

they groan, now that the novelty has worn off. And finally, there are those who consider drag decadent, perverse, reprehensible: "It's the end of Western civilization," a friend, an esteemed novelist whose work illumines the darkest parts of human nature, pronounced when I told her the subject of my research. Though I had no argument at the time, I knew that I disagreed. This book is the result of my efforts to figure out why.

The more I witnessed, the more convinced I became that people who dress in drag are acting on behalf of us all. The average guy may regard "gender" as a deadly subject, tedious and pedantic, the hobbyhorse of angry women and arrogant intellectuals out to undermine the life he has made. But not even the indifferent, who dismiss the gender debate, can escape it, and those who refuse to formulate their own ideas simply proceed according to somebody else's, guided by received notions, many of them contradictory. Implicit or stated, the terms in which we define masculinity and femininity are in fact so fundamental that they determine how we feel about ourselves and one another.

To a surprising extent, then, and in ways that might not be apparent at first glance, drag pertains to those of us whose everyday lives conform more closely to the norms. The man whose wife earns more money than he does, the woman who cuts her hair short and finds that men respond differently to her, the man who hesitates before opening the door for a woman, the woman who hesitates before opening the door for herself, the husband who stays home to take care of the children, the woman trying to decide whether to wear spike heels or flats for a first date, the parents who wonder whether a Barbie doll will skew their daughter's nascent sense of what a woman ought to look like—these people's concerns are fundamentally not all that different from the questions being addressed by most drag queens. In a nutshell: What is a woman and, by extension, what is a man? What are the requirements for credibility? What, if any, are the signs that can be trusted? When you strip away the conventions we've inherited, the extreme behavior that establishes the masculine and the feminine as polar opposites—the simpering and the blustering, the feigned helplessness and the compulsory strength, the hysteria and the stoicism—what's left?

The most immediate and obvious lesson that drag has to offer is that we need a new set of signals, that the old ones are no longer reliable. To the extent that we have fetishized femininity, it can be replicated by anyone. The lips, the high heels, the breasts, the hips—features that for most of our century (indeed, for most of history) have telegraphed the presence of a woman—have been appropriated by drag queens, and in all but the broadest cases, we mistake the decoy for the real thing: the illusion triumphs over the reality, the generic over the particular.

"When you meet a human being," Freud wrote, "the first distinction you make is 'male or female?' and you are accustomed to making the distinction with unhesitating certainty." Drag temporarily confounds us: we're unable to come up with the answer. Or sometimes we come up with the answer and then discover that we were wrong, in which case drag exposes our gullibility, provoking a sense of betrayal. More often than not, we feel betrayed by the drag queen, when in fact it is our own assumptions that have betrayed us.

In the seven years since I began this book, drag in America has gone from a downtown pastime in New York and a handful of other cities—a private joke among fashion designers, photographers, artists, filmmakers, and self-styled performers in search of an audience—to a national form of mainstream entertainment. Hollywood has produced a spate of movies in which much of the draw resides in seeing a regular guy like Robin Williams or a he-man like Wesley Snipes dressed as a woman. In the summer of 1997, the Film Society at Lincoln Center sponsored "What a Drag!," a summer festival for children, conceived by one Victoria Kabak, the ten-year-old winner of the center's "Kids' Curator Contest," who wrote in her entry that a film series on her theme would "teach people to be tolerant of others who are different." *Drag Dolls*, an album of famous contemporary drag queens rendered as paper dolls, has been published, to say nothing of any number of other books, including one, *A Field Guide to New York Drag Queens*, in the style of a manual for birdwatchers. John Berendt's *Midnight in the Garden of Good and Evil*, a long-running best-seller, has inspired at least one spin-off—the autobiography of the Lady Chablis, a drag queen who figures as its most vivid character. In 1997, k.d. lang issued an album called *Drag*. The following year, *Hedwig and the Angry Inch*, a rock musical, and Eddie Izzard, who calls himself "a male lesbian," played to sellout audiences in New York. Drag terminology has infiltrated the language: we use it to differentiate our various personas (my "party drag," my "business drag"); we describe someone having a temper tantrum as "wigged out." "Girlfriend" has become an honorific, bestowed in conversation, according to the Lady Chablis, on "a biological girl or any person who is gay, fem'nine, or open-minded."

In advertising, Linda Evangelista, the supermodel, appeared as both Romeo and Juliet in a campaign for Kenar. RuPaul was hired to represent Mac, the cosmetics line—a prestigious appointment in the tradition of Isabella Rossellini for Lancôme and Cindy Crawford for Revlon. John Cleese was photographed in drag, sporting a hat and pearls, in an ad for American Express.

Dennis Rodman and Howard Stern have shown up for personal appearances in full bridal regalia. Kurt Cobain wore a dress. In the summer of '97, as the concerted manhunt for Andrew Cunanaen, the serial killer suspected of murdering Gianni Versace, wore on, the *New York Post* touted the theory that he was eluding the FBI by dressing in drag. Specimens of manhood as disparate as Bono and Mayor Rudolph Giuliani have appeared in drag. "What next?" a friend asked recently. "Any day now, I expect to turn on the television and see Bill Clinton in drag."

Insiders argue that drag—real drag—is dead now or that, in order to survive this blitz of popular attention, it has gone underground. But if the zeal with which drag queens dressed up and went out seems in some sectors to be waning, the notion of drag has in one way or another insinuated itself into the realm of the average and the ordinary. With the Internet came the option of doing drag without the clothes. One man I know, a fifty-two-year-old novelist, frequents chat rooms and strikes up conversations about sex in the guise of a twenty-five-year-old lesbian—a pretext, his wife says dryly, that enables him to meet other fifty-two-year-old men masquerading as twenty-five-year-old lesbians.

Most men who dress in women's clothes, as I see it, fall into one of the following four categories: female impersonators, who do drag onstage as part of a performance (a distinguished tradition that includes the Hasty Pudding Club, Kabuki, John Kelly, Joey Arias, and Milton

Berle); transsexuals, who believe that they were born the wrong sex and set out to rectify that, with hormones and surgery; "cross-dressers," as they're now known in America—men (the majority of them straight) who dress in women's clothes, usually underwear and usually in private, often as a sexual turn-on; and, finally, the practitioners I'll call drag queens, who dress as women in public, on social occasions.

It is this last group that forms the basis of this book, however blurred the distinctions. Admittedly, the mid-century French photographer who specialized in portraits of himself in women's clothes—primarily lingerie—might be better classified as a cross-dresser. The cross-dressers who claim that their impulse to dress in women's clothes (and not only lingerie) is not erotic would theoretically qualify as drag queens. The performance artist—a woman—in drag as a man dressed as a woman invented her character for the stage, which would relegate her to the genus of female impersonator; but she also goes to parties as that character and so (according to my taxonomical criteria) deserves consideration as a drag queen.

What impressed me about drag when I embarked on this investigation was that it articulates men's idea of women, or one man's idea of women, or in some cases one man's idea of one woman in particular. These are women as seen by men—or as men would like to see them. The notion of a woman as a man's creation may have fallen out of favor, but its erotic appeal has never died. Charles Frederick Worth, Alfred Stieglitz, George Balanchine, and others molded women to their visions. The impulse is not gone, but in the current climate of political correctness, it has gone underground, with drag one of its few permissible outlets. I wanted to get a glimpse of the images of women that men carry in their minds—images, increasingly subject to self-censorship, that contain some private ideal. In an absurd, inbred reenactment of the artist in love with his muse, who becomes his description of her, a man can now incarnate the woman of his dreams: Pygmalion transforms himself into Galatea.

Eager for some perspective on drag as I knew it, I set out for other countries, becoming a tourist in an international subculture that, from the outset, seemed both remarkably foreign and oddly familiar. Wandering the back streets of eight drag capitals (New York included), I set out to catalogue the prevailing clichés of femininity and how they differ from one society to the next. I wanted to understand how the seemingly standard image of a guy in a dress might intersect with the changing idea of a woman in other cultures. Which aspects of drag were the universal themes and which aspects the local variations? Ian Buruma contends that "it is the expression of fantasies that often differs from one nation to another rather than the fantasies themselves."

Though the ideal varied, it must be said that the men I found who dress in drag most often became babes if not outright bimbos, bearing little resemblance to the ideal most women have set for themselves. So, in the interest of equal time, I enrolled in an introductory course for drag kings, teaching women how to dress as men, to satisfy my curiosity as to whether women, under similar circumstances, represented men as more three-dimensional, less stereotypical. Seasoned drag kings will look on our freshman endeavors as an abomination, lacking the seriousness with which they go about transforming themselves, and I hereby beg their pardon for giving them short shrift. But to my mind, women in drag on the whole lack the credibility and the audacity that make men in drag so provocative. We're inured to the thrill that the sight of Marlene Dietrich in a tuxedo inspired in her own time. After two generations of flat shoes and pantsuits, a woman in drag now looks not brazen or defiant or even titillating but completely harmless. In any case, the woman who dresses as a man in our time gains nothing by it; she has already acquired the liberty and the privileges that men's clothes confer. Whereas the man who dresses as a woman enters into a realm of experience that has been off-limits to him.

In the course of my travels, I acquired enormous respect for drag as a means of expression—for its eloquence and subtlety. I wanted the reader to meet the drag queens I met, to feel the force of their intelligence, to take in their personalities at close range. Since the start of my research, drag has evolved and much else has changed: bars have come and gone, club nights have moved or disbanded, the queen bee of New York night life (a woman) has been divorced and remarried, several of the subjects I interviewed have died. Even so, they and the circumstances in which I encountered them exist for me in a kind of continuous present, and that is the spirit in which I portray them here, in a cavalcade that spans this final decade of the so-called Century of Woman.

GIRLFRIEND

ABANDON

legal drag 1. *man who wears a dress when masquerading is permitted by law (Halloween, Mardi Gras, etc.). "I'm a legal drag until midnight—then I change back into a Marine."*

BRUCE RODGERS,
The Queens' Vernacular: A Gay Lexicon

....

On a steamy Saturday afternoon in February, the beach at Copacabana—a wide swath of white sand that separates the jumble that is Rio de Janeiro from the ocean—is covered with bodies, wall to wall, forming a low, rolling landscape of breasts, buttocks, and thighs. The local residents run the gamut from bronze to brown to black; the tourists, many of them recently arrived from countries up north, where it's winter, are conspicuously pale. Men and women wearing tiny string bikinis sunbathe with utter disregard for doctors' warnings about premature aging, about skin cancer. If those and other misfortunes befall the flesh, they'll befall it later. Here, the horizon extends no further than this evening's celebrations.

Nearby, the *banda d'Ipanema* makes its way through the neighborhood for which it is named. The streets, lined with palmettos and parked cars, seem too narrow to contain the snaking horde as it sweeps along everyone in its path—residents walking their dogs, delivery boys on bikes, children playing. A cook in his apron perches in the upstairs window of a restaurant to watch the motley parade as it passes. Santa Claus, Nefertiti, and Carmen Miranda are all represented, as well as a host of lesser-known characters outfitted in fishnet stockings, bright-colored tinsel pageboy wigs, feathers, and beads. A father carries a little girl who carries a bag of sequins, strewing them along the way.

One of four Carmen Mirandas—this one a businessman, he claims, who looks to be in his fifties, wearing platform shoes, a sarong skirt, and a headdress heaped with a pineapple, grapes, a watermelon, a minah bird, and a big red bow—zeroes in on a blond man in swim trunks and flip-flops. "What your name is?" Carmen Miranda ventures, in English.

Half a mile along the parade route, in a gesture of resignation that women know all too well, a man dressed in a blond wig, a white-eyelet midriff top, and a gingham skirt pauses by a tree and changes out of the high heels he's been wearing into a pair of flat espadrilles that he pulls from his wicker purse.

In 1965, when the *banda d'Ipanema* got its start, it was a fraction of its current size, and Ipanema's population was a mere third of what it is today. Albino Pinheiro, a businessman, organizes the *banda* and pays its expenses. Asked why, he replies that he does it "as a big joke." He says that this *banda* "was made for white people who don't have samba in their blood." There are other *bandas*, in other neighborhoods, but the *banda d'Ipanema* is undoubtedly the most famous, and it is particularly famous for the drag queens who every year constitute a sizable percentage of its ranks. Pinheiro thinks that the presence of drag queens during Carnaval is important to the spirit of the occasion. He describes his *banda* as "more democratic" than the others. These days, he says, nearly a thousand people turn out for it, and he takes evident pride in the fact that they come from all over Rio and beyond, not just Ipanema.

The city is littered with Carnaval gear, on sale at every corner for the benefit of those who haven't spent the past eleven months planning for these few days—tourists and anyone else getting into the spirit at the last minute. Stands in the market sell masks and wigs, paper boas, plastic fedoras with a feather inserted jauntily in the band. A display next to the cash register at the health food restaurant offers products that athletes use to increase their endurance. *"Energia total!"* the sign promises. Carnaval is a marathon, and the spectators, as well as the participants, need fortifying.

In recent years, a series of drag balls has sprung up around the scheduled events. The Gala G (formerly the Grand Gala Gay, until someone trademarked the word *gay* in Brazil) was launched in the mid-sixties in an old theater in downtown Rio by Guilherme Araujo, an agent for musicians and a concert manager. These days, the party is held on Tuesday, the last night of Carnaval—the eve of Ash Wednesday—on Sugarloaf Mountain, with guests traversing the last leg of the trip by funicular. Carnaval is the great equalizer, Araujo says, and his intent has always been to bring together all kinds of people: artists, actors, singers, society types—not only gay but straight as well, not only drag queens but "serious people," as he calls them, dressing up, in drag or in evening clothes, for the fun of it. Admission is by invitation only.

By Araujo's own account, the best years were from '81 to '87—he calls them "a golden time." Those were the days when he would contract interior decorators and set designers to create a fantasy decor, when two thousand people would come and Brazilian celebrities would mix with the international set that made the circuit from one party to the next, from London to Paris to New York to Rio. Attendance has fallen off since then, though Araujo's phone still rings constantly with desperate requests for tickets in the days just before the big night. But, he contends, the most significant change over the years has been in the party's atmosphere. At the start, it was much more private, closed to media coverage—the sort of place where somebody from an important family could go in drag and meet only friends and sympathetic strangers. Then the television crews arrived, and the Gala G has never been the same.

Nowadays, Araujo laments, people dress for the cameras, to get their attention. It's true, he admits, that there are many more tourists in town for Carnaval now, but they are not to blame for this change in the Gala G, he says. The guests who pride themselves on being outrageous are Brazilians, playing to a Brazilian audience, and although Araujo deplores what he calls the "vulgarity" they have introduced, he is resigned to it as a hallmark of the times in which we live. Araujo subscribes to the theory that there is no sex anymore, that AIDS has put a stop to it. There is, he says, only the *representation* of sex, which is everywhere, and this is what many drag queens have to offer; this is the basis of their fascination. We are living in an era of voyeurism, when people routinely make spectacles of themselves—a phenomenon that, he is quick to admit, has made his parties more telegenic. Still, there is an undertone of sadness or regret in his voice when he talks about the way the drag balls used to be and what they have become, now that "decadence" has set in and changed everything.

For year-round drag queens, Carnaval offers a pretext for extravagance. For others—men with wives and children, men who wouldn't be caught dead in a dress the other three hundred sixty-one days a year—Carnaval provides the license to be someone else, to do the things that someone else might do, someone unaccountable. Conventional male roles—the breadwinner, the pillar of the community—are temporarily suspended, then reclaimed just in time for Lent, that tunnel of piety. And God obligingly looks the other way. He turns his face from the glittering proceedings at the Sambadrome, from the beer-drenched goings-on at midnight in the streets, from the television, where the hedonistic Parade of the Virgin, in Orlinda, a small town in the northeastern state of Recife, is broadcast nationwide. Long and celebrated as the tradition of dressing in drag for Carnaval may be, however, it is not considered particularly dignified. In the space of a week in Rio, a visitor encountered some two dozen people who remembered men in dresses during the Carnavals of their childhoods but, remarkably, no one whose own father had ever dressed in drag—a phenomenon that calls to mind contemporary France, where everybody's father was in the Resistance.

Drag as practiced here mostly upholds the status quo, not only by ratifying the image of women as men like to see them but also, during Carnaval, by allowing men a brief vacation from a sometimes burdensome masculinity and its attendant responsibilities. A man may be in the masculine mode or, briefly, out of it completely; in either case, masculinity, as a concept, is preserved uncompromised and unadulterated.

When, in Brazil, drag subverts the prevailing sex roles by shaking the spectator's faith in the hallmarks of femininity, it is the full-time, wholehearted drag queens who do the subverting. Guys who put on a dress at Carnaval and leave their mustaches untouched, as if to make double-sure that the dress is read as a joke, call nothing whatsoever into question. Year-round drag queens in Rio dismiss the way straight men dress up during Carnaval as "bad drag," and in conversation they go to great lengths to set themselves apart from men decked out in party gowns borrowed for the occasion—men who don't even own a pair of high heels that they can call their own. For four days a year, everything is drag, and the important distinctions are not between those who do it and those who don't but between one kind of drag and another.

....

At the Sambadrome, a huge concrete arena on the outskirts of Rio de Janeiro, a sellout crowd has gathered on Sunday night for one of four Carnaval parades—the climax of a year's worth of planning and rehearsals. Essentially a parade ground put to use four days a year, the Sambadrome is itself a monument to Carnaval's importance in the life of this society: two steep banks of bleachers face each other across a mile-long strip of asphalt no wider than a boulevard, as if the architects, commissioned to design a sports stadium, had forgotten the playing field. At the top of the bleachers are glassed-in private boxes— a tier of penthouse suites leased by corporations and wealthy individuals. From the bottom of the canyon formed by the stands, one can look up and see the silhouettes of the men and women inside, framed by the windows.

In the dirt area near the gate, the samba schools assemble, lining up their floats amidst idling buses and rusted trucks. The hot-dog vendors fill orders at a clip as a line forms. Little girls dressed as angels, with marabou halos, weave their way through the crowd to their assigned positions. Newly hatched baby chicks—children wearing half a shell around their hips—fidget as they wait their turn. A harlequin on stilts, standing ready, crosses herself.

And then, suddenly, the waiting and the stage fright have run their course: it's time. The drummers telegraph the beat, and the dancers surge forward through the gates, onto the paved road. The floodlights are blinding. Each samba school—not really a school but a club of sorts—claims several thousand members, all of whom parade: dancers, musicians, brawny men to push the floats. Everybody sings. Each school presents a dozen or so floats that are triumphs of architecture, engineering, and window display. This particular year, there are, to name only a few: a float based on a Venetian theme, with gondolas protruding from the front; a locomotive; a grotto. It will take the procession roughly an hour to make its way from the entrance to the exit, all the way at the other end. Between schools, there are fireworks.

The women wear G-strings covered in sequins or fringed with beads, and beaded bras that harness their breasts, leaving them bare or, for modesty's sake, covering the nipples with a little scallop shell. Fat and thin, young and old, the women hurl themselves into the music, shimmying and twirling, confident that they have never looked more beautiful. A grandmother—nearly naked, wearing glasses—dances with radiant abandon. At the top of a multitiered float, an Art Nouveau pavilion with Tiffany-style stained-glass windows, stands a drag queen dressed in white fishnet stockings, a silver-and-crystal-beaded G-string, and a matching bra top that traces the outline of her breasts, with an enormous red feather fan attached to her back. She smiles and waves at the crowd; she looks the cameras right in the eye, while down below, on the street all around her, men, women, and children bob and sway, carried along on the frenzy unleashed by the beat of the drums.

Beauty here is an asset more precious than money. The latest victims of the rampant street crime that has frightened people into leaving their jewelry and their money at home are young women who are mugged for their hair, which is then sold on the black market and made into wigs and toupees. The women turn up on television, their hair hacked close to the scalp, and tell their stories, eliciting vast outpourings of sympathy from the viewing audience—sympathy that a missing watch or the loss of two weeks' pay would never inspire.

To be beautiful in Brazil, if you're a woman, is to have large hips and ample thighs—to be what Americans disparagingly call "broad across the beam"—with a small bustline. In a country where plastic surgery figures in the press as a national industry, with the tabloids full of reports of movie stars in town for face-lifts, the notion of resorting to heroic measures in order to look more attractive is widely accepted. Standing in line at a bank, a visitor overhears a secretary describing to her friend the details of her recent surgery to have her eyebrows lifted. The most popular procedure among Brazilian women, however, is breast reduction, in stark contrast to the statistics in the United States and many European countries, where, until the hazards of silicone implants recently came to light, women were signing up in droves for breast "augmentation." In Brazil, many of the patients undergoing surgery for breast implants are men: drag queens looking for a little more verisimilitude.

There are other ways to acquire breasts. Hormones and injectable silicone (as well as steroids) are deregulated and available over the counter, without a prescription, in most of Rio's drugstores. Customers can either be injected by the pharmacist or do it themselves, in private, at home. So, male chests are given a bosom; male hips and thighs, narrow and lean by nature, are filled out. Drag here is not confined to mere clothes. Bodies are altered to resemble more closely whatever it is they're dressed up to be. The long-term casualties of these methods are everywhere apparent: on the beaches, in bars and cafés, on the streets, there are bodies disfigured in bizarre, often grotesque ways, the result of silicone injections that have migrated over time. A jowly drag queen encountered in a bar during Carnaval complains bitterly that the silicone she used to give herself more prominent, aristocratic cheekbones has now fallen. Her friend, also in drag, hikes up the hem of her dress to show a visitor the pouchy deposits of silicone on the outsides of her thighs—more unsightly by far than the cellulite and the so-called saddlebags to which so many women fall prey. Deformity turns out to be the price paid all too often for some glorious but momentary physical transformation.

Transformista is the name most drag queens in Rio prefer to be called. Those who lip-synch in clubs label themselves "artists." But the standard slang for a transvestite is "doll," a word Brazilian drag queens use in referring to themselves, with evident pride in qualifying as a sex object. So much a part of Carnaval have the drag queens become that in 1992 the União da Ilha do Governador, one of the samba schools, lobbied for and won a third toilet in the rehearsal hall where the samba schools assemble before the parade: now there is one toilet for men, one for women, and one for dolls.

Carnaval coverage on television preempts prime-time shows and dominates the local news programs. Viewers all over the country tune in to the festivities at the Sambadrome, outside Rio, with commentary by celebrities as special hosts. When, in 1992, this prestigious appointment was conferred on Rogeria, a famous drag queen who works as a television actress and looks like a French starlet, circa 1960, the consensus among the drag queens in Rio was that the appointment signified not only the culmination of Rogeria's career to date but also a watershed in the history of Carnaval.

Once Carnaval is over and the frenzy subsides and society revokes the average guy's license to wear a dress until the same time next year, drag reverts to the diehards—the queens, full- or part-time, who frequent the beaches and the bars, who need no occasion. They are not inconspicuous. Every Sunday evening, a popular television show called *Programa Silvio Santos* feeds the national fascination with physical transformation, bringing a drag beauty contest of sorts into the homes of ordinary Brazilians. First comes the chorus of children singing, then the couples ballroom dancing, which flows seamlessly into the drag competition hosted by Silvio Santos himself, a Bob Barker type who is enough of a national celebrity that he once ran for president; he is also, as it happens, the owner of the station. If Santos's show is any indication, the line between the sexes seems to be more easily transgressed than any racial barrier in Brazil. (There are, incidentally, no black contestants, according to one faithful viewer.)

The first prize is money. Santos introduces the week's contestants by their male names before allowing them to use their female names, which he refers to as their "stage names." Every use of a female pronoun is politely, but firmly, corrected. Having demonstrated their talents by performing a musical number, the drag queens are interviewed. "Are you married or single?" Santos asks one contestant.

"Single," she—no, *he*—replies.

"Well," Santos says reassuringly, "maybe that will change after the show. After all, there are lots of beautiful young women watching this evening who would be very interested in you." The fact that the contestant is shot full of silicone, with breasts and hips, does not deter Santos in his upbeat promise of a proper, connubial future.

Many drag queens feel that Santos's show reflects fairly accurately the attitudes of Brazilian society as a whole: the fascination with drag, the fear and anxiety it inspires, the impulse to paper over its more menacing aspects and render it harmless and congenial. Jacob Braiterman, an American anthropologist who has lived in Rio and done research on the drag queens there, believes that this complex response is to some degree universal, by no means confined to

PLATE 9

PLATE 10

PLATE 11

PLATE 12

PLATE 13

PLATE 14

PLATE 15

PLATE 16

PLATE 17

PLATE 18

PLATE 19

PLATE 20

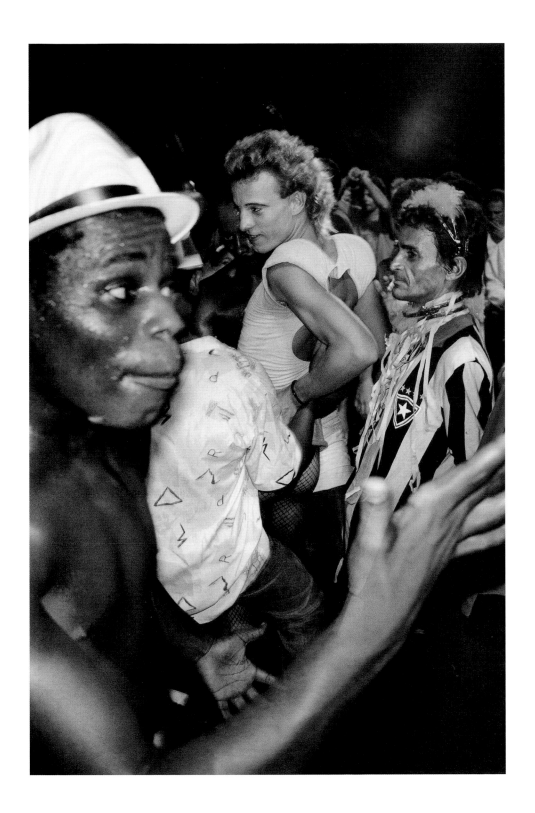

PLATE 21

PLATE 22

PLATE 23

PLATE 24

Brazil, and that it arises in the face of the paradox that drag queens represent—the unsettling combination of a submissive, feminine image and, just beneath the surface, masculine aggression, the perpetual threat of power held temporarily in check. "Chicks with dicks," they're called. "Drag queens, women, and gays," he says, "all live in a dominated position. They support straight male dominance and subvert it, at the same time." Braiterman rejects the romantic notion of Brazil as a sexually permissive society—an image propagated by travel agents and the music industry. Popular singers upheld as examples of stars who are universally revered despite their sexually checkered pasts, are, Braiterman insists, no different from Elton John and David Bowie.

Among the drag queens in Rio who take their calling seriously, a few have achieved a renown that extends all the way to the mainstream. People recognize Laura do Vison, for one, in the street. They've seen her on Silvio Santos's show and, Braiterman says, they respect her for the fact that she has made a middle-class life for herself, with a middle-class income: during the day, dressed as a man (though not particularly convincingly, according to one friend and fellow drag queen), she teaches civics in a public school; at night, she works in a club. In drag, she is exaggerated, cartoonish, with a mouth drawn too big and eyebrows traced too high, in clothes that reveal a thickset body.

Rogeria, for her part, commands admiration for the fact that, unlike most Brazilian drag queens, she actually sings (as opposed to lip-synching); she also speaks French. An air of European sophistication surrounds her. When Brazilian drag queens choose to impersonate a stock female character, it is often a French chanteuse, like Edith Piaf. Cochinelle, the famous French drag entertainer, lived for a time in Rio, where she had a thriving career in music halls and supper clubs, playing to an appreciative audience of middle-class, married couples.

The European overtones are crucial, conferring, as they do, a touch of class. Europe is, in fact, the eventual destination for many Brazilian drag queens, who have earned a reputation in Paris and in Rome as fearless, cut-rate prostitutes, standing by the side of the road and flashing passing motorists, wearing next to nothing under huge fur coats, like the heroines of a Helmut Newton fashion shoot. Eventually, they return home with a car they've bought with the money they've made and an Italian wardrobe, in the sober, conservative style worn by the upper-middle-class women of Milan.

But during Carnaval, at least, the overtones of old-world elegance are drowned out by the clamor of Hollywood kitsch, as dozens of drag queens in the streets, a *banda*, and an entire samba school pay tribute to Carmen Miranda. Guilherme Araujo calls her the patron saint of Brazilian transvestites, and though some local drag queens regard her cult as old-fashioned and tacky, her influence is unmistakable. In the middle of Flamingo Park, in a building that looks like a bunker, a small museum in her honor preserves a handful of her costumes, tattered now, and a meager collection of memorabilia. Postcards for sale in the souvenir shops depict her in spangled sarong skirts and platform shoes, in dresses cut away to reveal a bare midriff, her hands loaded with gigantic rings, her arms stacked with bracelets. Her hair is elaborate, piled high; her nails are long and lacquered crimson. The drawn-on arches of her eyebrows, the long fringe of her eyelashes, the enormous mouth, painted red, stretched in an exuberant smile, are all on a scale that seems slightly preposterous. Araujo says that Carmen Miranda was always popular with the gay audience in Brazil because she caricatured herself. That, in turn, made it easy for other people to imitate her. And, indeed, in photographs, she looks in retrospect like a drag queen dressed as Carmen Miranda.

These days, a sizable contingent of the drag queens who take her as their inspiration seem to regard her more as a concept or a category than as an icon. While the literal-minded slavishly re-create, say, Marilyn Monroe, the would-be Carmen Mirandas have gone off in another, increasingly abstract direction. Late at night along the waterfront in Copacabana, when people in town for Carnaval take to the streets, there are dozens of cornucopia headdresses bobbing in time to the samba beat broadcast by loudspeakers hooked up to a truck with a portable generator. The fruit is sequined, or made of tulle, or mixed with packaged groceries; the hair is bigger, wired into bizarre configurations; the platform shoes are higher than ever, covered with mirrors, festooned with plastic cherries; the jewelry is clunkier and more outrageous. Carmen Miranda is cast as the champion of fads in bad taste, including some, like Happy Face earrings, that she didn't live long enough to witness. Wearing ruffled bell-bottoms and an off-the-shoulder midriff top, and balancing an entire banana tree on the top of her head, one initiate in the cult crosses the street, bringing the bumper-to-bumper traffic to a halt. The drag queens play with Carmen Miranda's trademarks, spinning out variations that digress more and more from the original, keeping her alive each year by making her new.

The drummers for the *banda d'Ipanema*, scattered at intervals throughout the crowd, broadcast a throbbing samba beat. Two men in bridal gowns dance along frenetically, in unison. If what most men do when they dress up for Carnaval qualifies as "bad drag," here are two examples of it. One of them sports a mustache; both are outfitted in dresses with off-the-shoulder necklines, the latest style in Brazilian bridal fashions. Exulting in the rhythm, in the atmosphere of abandon, they move along like two escapees from the altar. And no wonder. Despite Rio de Janeiro's reputation as a favorite destination on the sex-tourism circuit, as a libertarian playground where anything goes, statistics indicate that most Brazilians marry in their early twenties, if not sooner, and embark straightaway on a life of bourgeois respectability. One of the two brides who have come out this afternoon with the *banda*—the one wearing the pearl-encrusted headdress with the pink tulle veil—says that he is from a small town near Pelotas, in Rio Grande del Sud, where he is married, with three children, aged eighteen, fifteen, and fourteen. Nobody there knows that he is gay, he says, but four days a year, for Carnaval, he comes here and lives out his fantasies. His best friend (and his cohort on this occasion) is the son of the owner of the local bridal shop. Together, they travel to Rio and model the gowns that every girl back home dreams of wearing for her own personal coronation, her fairy-tale wedding, the day her long-awaited life as a woman begins.

ACTIVISM

If I were now to see a woman sitting with her knees clamped together, one hand on her hip and the other lightly touching her back hair, I should think, "Either she scored her last social triumph in 1926 or it is a man in drag." Perhaps "camp" is set in the 'twenties because after that differences between the sexes—especially visible differences—began to fade.

QUENTIN CRISP,
The Naked Civil Servant

Many, if not most, of the people who come to Berlin come looking for decadence, and, generally speaking, Berlin obliges. Their expectations have been inspired by a late-night glimpse of *The Blue Angel* on cable television and by *Cabaret*, the movie or the Broadway show, or even, in the case of those inclined to books, by the Christopher Isherwood stories on which the show was based. The tourists carry in their minds a vague image of a windowless, smoke-filled room in which risqué musical numbers are staged for the benefit of world-weary audiences. Joel Grey is there, and Marlene Dietrich, dressed in a man's tuxedo. Now that it has served as material for popular entertainment, the Weimar Republic has been lifted from its context in history and reduced to one big nightclub.

It is not, however, a nightclub bearing much, if any, resemblance to the ones that animated Berlin in the early part of the century, when general-interest magazines listed some twenty bars as transvestite hangouts of various descriptions, popular with artists, intellectuals, and members of "high society." The Kleist-Kasino and the Eldorado were among the most famous; the Platen Society was renowned for its "literary" atmosphere. Though most bars were short-lived and the turnover was brisk, the Mikado, which opened in 1907, became something of an institution and remained in business for twenty-five years. At the Flottwell Klause, entertainment was provided by a pianist and a violinist. According to two visitors who recorded their impressions, there was little or no smoking or drinking (indulgences regarded as "manly"): "Those who linger here do not wish to be reminded that in their life outside they are forced to appear as men. They love lemonade and ices; they love everything that is otherwise enjoyed by ladies in pastry shops." In the early thirties, one of the city's most notorious transvestites, who went by the name of Voo-Doo, opened her own bar, which was soon filled with a fashionable crowd embarking on the latest trend: androgyny.

What Berlin is in a position to deliver in the way of decadence these days is considerably less conspicuous and picturesque. As the new capital of the unified Germany, the city takes itself seriously. Construction sites spring up at every turn, the skyline dominated by the profiles of huge cranes towering over the surrounding buildings. The new Berlin—the official Berlin, preoccupied with its public image—has no patience with this hankering for degeneracy and is loath to indulge it, unless the indulgence takes the sanitized form of a plastic monument to a theme-park past, one that doesn't much concern or even interest the local citizens.

The shows at Dollywood, at Berliner Gasthaus, at the handful of other nightclubs that cater to tourists in the nineties and figure on the list of every hotel concierge, all run together in the mind into a single, interminable, stupefying spectacle. There is the opening number from *Cabaret*, following the film's choreography to the letter, with the emcee played by a woman, in drag as Joel Grey. The hit song from *Cats* is memorable only for the oafish blond man, center stage, who is concentrating so hard on the dance routine that he forgets to move his mouth and lip-synch along with the original cast album. "I Will Survive" is sung by a man in a tight red evening gown, embroidered with sequin flames and slit to the thigh, who delivers his rendition of Gladys Knight's rendition of Gloria Gaynor's rendition; his bravura culminates in a final pose, in silhouette against the backdrop, betraying a slight paunch and a lack of any hips whatsoever. Two male acrobats in tutus clamber to the top of a trembling human pyramid. A drag angel in tap shoes hammers out a stop-time chorus of "Tea for Two." Then there is the bathetic finale, in which the entire cast returns, holding hands and mouthing the words to "I Am What I Am," from *La Cage aux Folles*.

With the exception of a token drag queen hired by the management to stand at the bar, the clientele is overwhelmingly average-looking. They have come in groups of four or six or eight, subdivided into couples. They guffaw at the sight gags. They talk over the music, in Dutch, English, Italian, Danish, Czech. The only voices in German belong to the waiters, taking orders for beer and schnapps.

The entertainment served here is drag lite: it looks like drag, but most of the content has been removed. The drag is primarily an allusion to hedonism, referring spectators back to their own fantasy—the fantasy that propelled them here. They get a whiff of decadence once removed and then go home. Sanctimoniously, and with a heavy hand, the clubs invoke the spirit of Weimar, as if it could confer authenticity on these paltry, rote proceedings.

Asked about the current state of drag, most Berliners cite the Tuntenball as evidence that it's thriving. An annual event inaugurated in the late seventies, the Tuntenball has swelled to an estimated six thousand people, of which four hundred or so are drag queens and the rest mostly businessmen and their wives, a few senators, the local TV newscasters; corporations buy up tickets in bulk and take out ads in the souvenir program. This commercial-scale photo op is all that remains of a lively tradition that extends at least as far back as the late 1800s, to the so-called gentlemen's balls—many of them private affairs that took place in the home of some well-to-do host. A book published in 1900 offers an account of young men in extravagant gowns acting the part of the ladies until, in the early morning hours, real women (from the *demi-monde*, the author asserts) appeared and began vying with the transvestites for the other men's attention. The transvestites won out. During that same time, the Berlin Philharmonic sponsored a biennial event—a ball attended by some twenty-five hundred women, the majority of them in drag; no men were admitted. By 1907, according to other sources, there were several drag balls a week, sometimes several in one night, at the height of "the season," and though the entrance fee was steep, they were quite popular, particularly with foreign tourists.

It is not so much that drag in Berlin has died down as that the attitudes that gave rise to drag in all its former glory have largely died out. Nearly one hundred years have gone by since Magnus Hirschfeld and other doctors conferred their clinical blessing on homosexuality and transvestism, rescuing these conditions from the stigma of criminal behavior and reassigning them to the realm of psychology. The effects were far-reaching. Though most Germans at the start of this century stopped short of condoning homosexuality and drag, the social climate brought on by the research of Hirschfeld and his colleagues was tolerant to an extent that would be unthinkable today. In 1908, General Count Hulsen-Haeseler, in drag as a ballerina, suffered a heart attack while performing an after-dinner dance routine for the kaiser and fellow members of his hunting party. Homosexuality in the kaiser's entourage was in fact common knowledge, and Germany then had the largest homosexual rights movement of any European country. In the aftermath of World War I, this assertiveness was given new impetus by the sense that the existing order was disintegrating. The bonds the veterans had forged in the trenches and the sober realization that death is too high a price to pay for machismo must have made ordinary citizens more receptive.

Despite the avid voyeurism that seems to have been at the heart of twenties nightlife in Berlin, the evidence indicates that most drag queens of the time did not set out to shock or even to call attention to themselves; good drag was credible and inconspicuous. In 1927, *Die Insel*, a magazine published in Berlin, sponsored a contest, announced in its pages. "Prize question: man or woman?" the announcement declared, beneath a picture of a stolid-looking individual whose hair is combed back off the face, who is wearing a high-necked black dress and a single strand of pearls. "We are offering five money-prizes for the correct answer to this question." An article published in 1929 in *Die Freundin*, a magazine for transvestites, dispensed practical advice for those who regularly dressed in drag. Among the suggestions:

• Be frank with friends and close acquaintances. This will have the added benefit of assuring you appropriate ladies' gifts on birthdays, etc.
• Go out at night in the company of a man to gain self-confidence.
• Never seek out doctors who try to cure you from your "sufferings" through hypnosis and the like.—Consult a "specialist" and seek to

obtain a medical document prepared on a scientific basis. The mere possession of the document will offer great comfort to those who are fearful and in case of any conflict with the police it will be of great service and will help to solve any crisis smoothly.

Applications for permission to wear women's clothes in public required a medical document and were rarely granted. But *Die Freundin* maintained that it was relatively easy for a transvestite to obtain written confirmation that the police were aware of his predilection and that there were no charges against him. The official policy was one of protection, and the drag balls of the twenties took place under the watchful eye of undercover cops until 1933, when homosexual meeting places were closed by the Nazis and the Bund für Menschenrecht (the League for Human Rights), which had championed transvestites, abruptly abandoned their cause.

What happened to drag during the war years is a mystery that most Berliners seemingly prefer to leave unsolved. History in Germany being discontinuous, the collective memory takes for granted that narrative—even (or particularly) personal narrative—breaks down at certain junctures. The war was one. The Wall is another. In Berlin, most of the few drag queens old enough to have lived through the war—like Strapsharry, for instance, a.k.a. Harry Toste, who is not a transvestite, he says, merely a drag performer—are notably vague when it comes to that chapter of their lives. The younger drag queens content themselves with the recent past for background. As far as they're concerned, the glory days weren't the twenties but the late seventies and early eighties, when there were several competing clubs that didn't play to tourists; when Romy Haag was running a disco and the entertainment there was voted best production of the year by a panel of drama critics; when she publicly heralded the arrival of a new generation, for whom, she claimed, gender would be immaterial. ("Are you a man or a woman?" a reporter for *Der Spiegel* asked her. "Yes," she replied.) And then she moved to Hamburg.

The younger drag queens in Berlin still talk about the fashion show that Bev Stroganov organized in 1989, at the "Offline," an avant-garde fashion fair, now defunct. They reminisce about how "professional" the presentation was and how "successful," demonstrating not that men could pass convincingly as women but that men could model women's clothes every bit as well—that the clothes would suffer nothing in the translation. The drag fashion shows of the twenties, many of them on a large scale, are too remote to be of interest to this generation. Besides, those events were usually organized around a mission, namely, to instruct transvestites in dressing tastefully and "fitting in"—a mission that doesn't sit too well with members of the current scene. The criterion of credibility, which once inspired magazine contests and baffled readers, no longer holds sway. The sense of women being beaten at their own game is rare here. Drag in the hands of this new generation belongs to a certain category of expression that in English has come to be known as "in-your-face," and the drag queens who have pioneered this premise are proud of it. If the sight of a man in a dress makes people uncomfortable, if it forces them to reexamine beliefs that they've cherished since childhood, then the goal has to some degree been accomplished. To the extent that femininity is an illusion, drag in Berlin often makes use of the illusion only to discredit it, directing the viewer's attention in the end to the realm of ideas, where some vital truth resides—there on the far side of appearances, which in any case are not to be trusted.

....

"I am not a drag queen, I am a work of art," Martin Ostrowsky asseverates right off, just after "hello" and a handshake. Drag is not in his case what it might appear to be. He wants to prevent people from coming to any mistaken conclusions based on the bridal gown he wears, the long gloves, the tulle stole, the white pumps. "I have the outfit of a drag queen, of course," Ostrowsky says, "but I take something which has for the normal mind a very low connotation and elevate it to the highest level imaginable—which for me is art." He wears the dress, he explains, because he doesn't want to be seen instantly as a man; he wears no wig because he doesn't want to be taken for a woman. To his mind, his work has the greatest potential for expression when the role he plays is neither female nor male, when he represents simply "a fellow member of our species." He characterizes his work as primarily performance art and painting, making use on occasion of sculpture, mixed media, environments, photography. Much of Ostrowsky's work—be it still lifes or landscapes or anything else—bears the same title: "Königen Luise," Queen Louise.

Most Germans, when they hear "Königen Luise," think of the Prussian queen by that name, a beloved figure in their history. Born in 1776, she acquired a far-reaching reputation as one of the most beautiful women of her time. In 1807, one year after Napoleon had conquered Prussia, Queen Louise went to him in Tilsit, fell to her knees, and asked him to release her country; he refused. Three years later, she died at the age of thirty-four, thereby attaining the status of a tragic heroine. Ostrowsky calls her "the Marilyn Monroe of her era." When at last in 1815 Prussia overthrew Napoleon, Queen Louise came to be regarded as the mother of her country, a symbol of hope and beauty. "I have nothing to do with that historical queen," Ostrowsky says, after having recounted her biography in some detail. "It's just a name I take, a name that people know, and I do something new with it."

Ostrowsky has been presenting himself as Königen Luise ("a symbol of purity," he says, "of the absolute ideal") since 1982. In the spring of 1991, dressed in his bridal gown and his white pumps, Ostrowsky walked the so-called death strip of the Berlin Wall—a former buffer zone presided over by abandoned watchtowers, cordoned off with barbed wire. For the first time since the Wall had come down, the area was opened to pedestrians, and Berliners turned out in droves to see where desperate citizens of the East had been gunned down in their attempts to escape. Every few days, over the course of five months, Ostrowsky traveled the narrow footpath that bisects the barren swath of land, its soil poisoned by DDT. In all, he estimates, he covered one hundred sixty-five kilometers. He stopped and talked to the people he met along the way—people who thought he must be mad—explaining to them that this was art. There was, he recalls, a spirit of mutual discovery in the air, as people who had been living on opposite sides of the Wall encountered one another, their foreign neighbors. Ostrowsky's journey was documented in a series of black-and-white photographs, exhibited at the Neuer Berliner Kunstverein and assembled in a book entitled *Königen Luise on the Wall Strip*. There are pictures of Königen Luise at the entrance to the tunnel there, with the high-rise buildings of East Berlin looming above the Wall in the background; of a self-portrait bust of Ostrowsky, cast in silver gypsum turned black and topped by a gold tiara, with KÖNIGEN LUISE engraved on the pedestal's base; of Königen Luise kneeling in an East Berlin street, praying in the shadow of the TV tower; of Königen Luise posed in front of the Soviet tank parked at the entrance to Berlin; of Königen Luise lying, in her pristine white dress, in the dirt on top of Hitler's bunker. "What terror went out from this place!" Ostrowsky says. "I felt the crying, the shouting, the ranting."

One year after the event, he says that it would be impossible to re-create his performance, so much have relations between the East and West in Germany soured since. The curiosity has been replaced by animosity—by disappointed economic hopes on the one hand, by resentment over the economic burden of unification on the other. Ostrowsky regards the photographs as relics of a brief and precious moment that has passed. Still, his work as Königen Luise continues, with a series of performances that take death as their subject. As Königen Luise, he attends gallery openings; she has become a familiar character on the streets of Berlin. Ostrowsky's other performances—the time he dressed as a beggar and made the rounds of an opening, panhandling, for instance, or the time he painted in front of an audience, using a dildo as a brush—have met with less enthusiasm. But the response to Königen Luise has been warm. She disarms people, she irritates them, she gets their attention. And then, Ostrowsky says, he can speak to them.

[There is] a custom widely spread among savages, in accordance with which some men dress as women and act as women throughout life. These unsexed creatures often, perhaps generally, profess the arts of sorcery and healing, they communicate with spirits, and are regarded sometimes with awe and sometimes with contempt, as beings of a higher or lower order than common folk.

SIR J. G. FRAZIER,
The Golden Bough

Among her peers, drag queens in their twenties and early thirties, Bev Stroganov is a controversial figure. She is famous for her costumes, which she sews herself: gowns that her fellow drag queens describe, sometimes dismissively or grudgingly, as "gorgeous." She will buy, say, twenty meters of pink brocade and make dresses for herself and for her friends. Bev ordinarily arrives at parties accompanied by a retinue. She is, it is unanimously agreed, handsome as a man and beautiful as a woman. And that, Matthias Frings believes, is the problem. A writer and the host of gay talk shows on radio and television, Frings is a veteran of the "off scene" in Berlin—the clubs and bars and theaters, concentrated in the area called Kreuzberg, that serve as an alternative to the city's cultural mainstream. He diagnoses the prevailing attitude toward Bev as part skepticism, part jealousy.

Bev's contemporaries profess a certain righteous disgust with the notion that a drag queen, like a woman, should be beautiful. Kaspar Kameleon, for one, has seen that kind of drag in New York, and he regards it as a missed opportunity. "I was a little shocked that the drag there was so feminine," he says, "with everyone trying to be the perfect woman. That is so conservative—so conformist, so strictly faithful to the female role model."

Ichgola Androgyn speaks for herself and for the drag queens who are her friends when she says, "In Berlin, we set out to make ourselves ugly." Here, the politics of the women's movement intersect with what Frings calls "the theater of insult," a trend in the performing arts that is particularly, if not exclusively, German. Just as a woman is no longer obliged to ingratiate herself to the world by means of her appearance, a performer is no longer obliged to entertain. A woman may go so far as to defy people to like her, dressing in clothes that constitute a deliberate affront to their taste; similarly, in recent theatrical productions, actors abuse the audience—spitting on them, calling them names. Frings traces these acts of aggression to the Germans' deep-seated mistrust of beauty—to their conviction that, far from beauty and truth being one and the same, beauty is in fact a *diversion* from the truth, a trap laid by the forces of evil to sidetrack the righteous man.

Among drag queens, at least, this cult of ugliness is not simply perverse but deeply political. "We are gay," Ichgola declares, "and we use drag for our gay interests—to call attention to our projects, to send a message to the public." She estimates that, all told, there are anywhere from twenty to thirty drag queens in Berlin who take part in this activism. They constitute a sort of family within the larger family that revolves around the Schwutz, the local gay center that hosts tea dances and films and lectures and serves as a clearinghouse for information of particular concern to the community.

The Schwutz has been a forum for drag since the mid-seventies, providing a stage free for the taking. Even now, drag queens who have no aspirations to performing step up on the stage of the Schwutz and sing songs—really sing, not just lip-synch. Ichgola, for one, loathes the convention, rampant in America, whereby a drag queen belts out "I Am What I Am" in someone else's voice. She and her friends consider their numbers an extension of their drag personas, as the chance to bring a little content to what might otherwise become an empty exercise in form. Ichgola says that though her "act" changes from one week to the next, the goal—to pose questions—remains constant. "I ask, 'What is a woman? Why do women wear high heels and bare their legs, and men don't? Why must a woman color her face, and not a man?' "

Ichgola believes that most women go to these inordinate lengths, which we accept as normal, for men's sake, not for their own. Still, she resists the suggestion that the drag she and her friends have pioneered is, in its own way, strenuously feminist. Let the feminists fend for themselves. "I hate their hardness," she says. Besides, she adds, with an apparent lack of irony, most of the women who subscribe to the feminist movement in Germany are lesbians.

The kind of drag that Ichgola and her cohorts do is not very old: she traces its origins to a group of drag queens who banded together in 1985 and called themselves Ladies' Neid—Ladies' Envy. Though other drag queens had dressed in such a way that they intentionally betrayed the fact that they were men, the members of Ladies' Neid made no pretense of looking like a woman; they were guys in dresses, patently gay and determinedly public, refusing to confine their drag to the safe haven of the gay community. Ichgola recalls that most gay men in Berlin were opposed to this new kind of drag, not only for fear of the flamboyant image it conveyed to the wider public but also, quite simply, because it was ugly. Acceptance came slowly, and only then, she believes, primarily as a result of the home-care station for AIDS patients that the drag queens instituted. She and Ovomaltine and Tima die Göttliche and other cohorts make the rounds of Berlin, doing housework for people with AIDS, delivering meals—dressed in drag.

In drag, they also stage demonstrations, sometimes no larger than a group of three, to protest the government's policies or society's prejudices. Ichgola says that she and her friends can't bring themselves to condone the practice of "outing" that has taken hold in America, where the gay community has exposed movie stars and athletes and politicians who had kept their homosexuality secret. But the right to privacy, as far as these drag queens are concerned, expires at death, and so they have engaged in several instances of what they call "historical outing." At the reinterment of Frederick the Great, in 1991, they turned out for the ceremony at Sans Souci, his palace in Potsdam. There they were, in the way of the television cameras: a dozen drag queens in historical dress whose presence announced to the German people what they didn't want to know, that this king, of whom they are so proud—this king who made Prussia great—was gay. Not surprisingly, Ichgola says, the response was hostile.

There is drag in Hamburg and in other cities in Germany, but Ichgola is persuaded that Berlin is the only possible home for the drag she and her friends practice. They have come from all over the country, from "villages where we didn't fit in," she says. "I am a Berliner," she continues, "insofar as I can say that only here am I able to live and develop." To Ovomaltine's mind, drag in Berlin today must be political, if only because the city itself is a political experiment. "As a German, born a German, I cannot tell you that I am proud of being German— instead, I must call myself 'cosmopolitan.' A Frenchman can tell you that he is proud of being French, and that's all right. But in Germany, this sort of remark is taboo, because of our history and because of our role in the new united Europe."

Poised between an ignominious past and an illustrious future, Berlin in the wake of the Wall's dismantling seems to occupy a historical no-man's-land not unlike the strip that formerly served as a buffer between the East and the West. Once again, the city has become a destination for the imagination. In the Weimar era, the attraction was to a place where people could explore or (more often) watch others explore the secret recesses of their psyches. Today, the romantic impulse that propels immigrants and tourists to Berlin is considerably different: a response to a certain sense of momentous possibility, of imminent transfiguration set against the detritus and the decay. Failure and mistaken notions of all kinds may be—must be—transcended; a person, like this city, could put the past behind and become someone else.

Among the trendy clubs that sprang up early on in the eastern sector were the Palace of Tears, in a building formerly used as a screening area for people leaving for the West, and E-Werk, in Hitler's bombproof electrical generating plant. Set in Berlin, the video for "One," a hit song by U2, features Bono and other members of the Irish band—some of rock and roll's most prominent sex symbols—in drag. It is hard to imagine the same video with Dublin, U2's hometown, or for that matter even Paris or London, as a backdrop. Berlin's search for identity is, to Ovomaltine's way of thinking, the collective aspect of a quest that is specifically German—a quest in which, she believes, drag in our time plays an indispensable role.

The trip from what was West Berlin to the eastern suburb of Mahlsdorf—the first leg by train and the second by streetcar—is over an hour long and made to seem even longer by the drastic changes the landscape undergoes along the way. Abruptly, at the crossing of the former border, a gray desolation sets in, a sense of chaos and ruin that the eventual appearance of random grass patches and an occasional tree does nothing to alleviate. One gathers by the look of things that zoning legislation did not hold much sway in the German Democratic Republic. The neighborhood that Charlotte von Mahlsdorf proudly calls home is a jumble of residential and industrial buildings, one on top of the other, interspersed with weedy vacant lots. The road is narrow and deserted, and her house, a former country mansion, is set perpendicular, cramped in such a way that the visitor is obliged to sneak up on it from the side, by means of a narrow passage. At dusk, there are no lights in any of the windows.

In response to a knock on the door at the top of the stairs, footsteps sound, growing louder as they approach. Finally, the door is opened by a figure hard to make out in the gloom—the maid, evidently, in a housedress, a bib-front apron, and the sort of lace-up shoes with stocky heels that people's grandmothers used to wear. She makes a sweeping gesture with her arm, a welcome into the dark that lies just inside the door, from which she will presumably conduct us to the mistress of the house. But she holds her ground and introduces herself. Her handshake—a man's firm, hearty grasp—confirms that this is not the maid but Charlotte von Mahlsdorf herself.

Through the blackness lies a rear parlor illuminated by two table

lamps, which reveal Charlotte to be solidly built, with a craggy face—
a strong nose, a square jaw, a prominent chin, a mouth drawn in a
firm though not unkind straight line. Her strawlike white hair is
parted on the side. She is wearing a demure double strand of pearls,
and no makeup.

Born Lothar Berfelde, in 1928, Charlotte dressed as a girl from an
early age; she has dressed as a woman, full-time, throughout her
adulthood. "I am a woman in the body of a man," she says, but hastens to add that she is not a transsexual. A sex change would be "unnecessary" in her case, she contends. "It is enough for me to dress
in a woman's clothes." She loves dusting and polishing the massive
sideboards, the bric-a-brac, the neo-Gothic dining-room suite, the
hand-carved walnut neo-Renaissance-style chairs that comprise her
collection of furniture and household objects from the Grunderzeit, a
twenty-year-long period defined as beginning in 1880. She takes visitors on a tour, playing for them a vintage polka on the Edison gramo-
phone, demonstrating the turn-of-the-century potato peeler. The
house itself, a manor built in 1780, had been slated for demolition
when Charlotte moved in, in 1959. She persuaded the East German
government to spare it and restored it with her own hands to its
present condition, as a private museum (the only private museum in
the GDR). Her knowledge of woodworking, she says, she learned from
a furniture restorer; the techniques for repairing clocks and mechani-
cal music devices, she acquired during an apprenticeship early on in
her career as a curator. Charlotte traces her fondness for the period
she has chosen as her specialty to her granduncle's house, where she
passed the only halcyon moments of an otherwise turbulent childhood. In the nine rooms that serve as a showcase for the articles she
has so lovingly assembled, many of them mass-produced and not especially precious or expensive, she has painstakingly re-created the
decor of the period, according to her vivid memories. "I live here exactly as a housewife would have lived here, one hundred years ago,"
she claims proudly.

Given all that has transpired in Germany since the bourgeois slumber of the Grunderzeit, there is something particularly poignant about
Charlotte's heroic efforts to re-create an era when life here was more
serene. The nostalgia for safety, which in other people often manifests
itself in yearnings for the styles—the clothes, the furniture—that pre-

vailed during their childhood, in Charlotte's case has been obliged to vault backward over two generations, some forty years beyond her birth. Her own early memories are mostly traumatic, dominated by an abusive, gun-wielding Nazi father—whom she killed one night in his sleep, she says matter-of-factly (she was sentenced to four years in a reformatory). As a youth, Charlotte found an important ally in her Aunt Luise, a female-to-male transvestite, who gave her a copy of Magnus Hirschfeld's landmark book, *Die Transvestiten* (The Transvestites), as a present and cautioned her about wearing women's clothes in public, given the shifting political winds.

Charlotte recalls an incident one evening in 1943, when she was fifteen or sixteen, walking with her best friend, both of them in drag, down the main street in Friedrichshafen: they were stopped by a Hitler Youth patrol and taken to the local police station for violating curfew. Under interrogation, Charlotte and her friend refused to give their names—which were, of course, male—for fear of the repercussions. After several hours spent in a holding cell, they finally relented, at which point the police stripped them of their clothes and whipped them. The other boy's mother was called and warned that if she couldn't raise her son correctly, he would be taken away from her—a threat that Charlotte and her friend later understood to be an unspoken reference to the work camp at Sachsenhausen, where the Nazis consigned transvestites and homosexuals. When Charlotte thinks of Sachsenhausen, she says now, she thinks of a drag queen she knew, an acquaintance who died in 1984, who spent the better part of the war at Sachsenhausen and told Charlotte stories about the transvestites' experiences there: about how many of them were raped and one of them castrated; about how she survived because an officer selected her for a job in the kitchen, thereby sparing her the hard labor that the other prisoners were forced to perform, in a stone quarry.

Charlotte offers a vivid account of her own narrow escapes, including a run for her life through the streets of Berlin as Soviet planes strafed the city—all the while dressed in a girl's coat, a girl's shoes, and stockings. In the war's final days, she was found, hiding out alone in a bomb shelter, by the SS. They asked her age. Sixteen, she said, not thinking, though in fact her birthday had just passed and, being seventeen, she had reached the age at which all German boys were required to enlist in the army. The police officers instructed her to set down the bag she was carrying, which contained half a loaf of bread and an alarm clock that Charlotte regarded as her "talisman"; they ordered her to face the wall and put her hands against it. "Are you a boy or a girl?" they asked her, as they drew their pistols and took aim. "I thought, *If they shoot, a boy is dead, and a girl is dead, too— what's the difference?*" Charlotte recalls. "So I said that I was a boy." At that moment an army officer came upon the scene and demanded to know what was going on. "We don't want to gun down school-children," he scolded the police, and sent Charlotte on her way.

One by one, the clubs and cabarets where homosexuals and trans-vestites had gathered before the war were raided and closed. Char-lotte recalls one such restaurant, the Mullerkritze, where toward the end of the war the proprietor saved the lives of forty-some transves-tites who would otherwise have been arrested for not being in uni-form. Drag balls continued to be held in private homes, according to Charlotte, "but it was always dangerous to attend, because you never knew where there might be an informer."

Up until the opening of the Wall, Charlotte had always exercised her penchant for dressing as a woman in the shadow of one repressive regime or another. She believes that it was easier to live as a transves-tite in the western sectors of Berlin. East Berlin, she says, was not so tolerant. In 1974, "authorities" sent by the state to inspect her mu-seum levied a tax on its contents—an impossible amount, a pretext for evicting her on personal and political grounds, she contends, because she was considered "an undesirable." Charlotte prevailed by giving away most of the museum's contents to its visitors, emptying fourteen of the twenty-three rooms, so that there would be nothing left to tax. As for her fellow citizens, they ignore her or they eye her quizzically or, in some cases, they greet her cordially: having returned to Mahls-dorf, her hometown, Charlotte now finds herself a local celebrity.

She is also something of a heroine among Berlin's gay rights ac-tivists. In 1992, she was awarded the Cross of the Order of Merit by the German government for her contributions toward the furthering of sexual freedom. The following year, she appeared as the star of a documentary film about her life, *Ich bin meine eigene Frau* (I Am My Own Woman), in which Rosa von Praunheim, the German director (another man who has likewise taken a woman's name, though he is not a drag queen), uses actors to dramatize certain of the more picturesque episodes (with Ichgola Androgyn in the role of Charlotte as a young adult). Charlotte regularly opens her house to members of the gay community for lectures, meetings, and social gatherings. In 1991, she gave a garden party, with some eighty people dancing in her backyard. "We thought we were finally safe," she recalls, "once the GDR had been dissolved." Instead, they were attacked by a band of teenage skinheads, who beat them with wooden bats and iron pipes. Charlotte blames the church for the Germans' prejudices against transvestites. The Nazis appropriated religion and used it for their own purposes, and then, after the war had ended, the transvestites and homosexuals were never rehabilitated; they never regained the rights they had had prior to the war. "It is one hundred years since Magnus Hirschfeld said that transvestism is no crime, that it must be seen as a psychological phenomenon," Charlotte laments, and yet since then the circumstances in Germany have grown worse, not better.

The longstanding tensions between transvestites and homosexuals still exist in Berlin. Charlotte recalls that before the war they viewed each other as enemies and tattled on each other to the police. To her mind, this is because, regardless of the situation, society always sees the transvestite as the woman, and society—even that microcosm of society that is the gay community—is relentlessly patriarchal. "Woman is Part Two," Charlotte says. "She is God's afterthought." Homosexuals look on transvestites as women, Charlotte explains, and therefore transvestites are discriminated against in homosexual society just as women are discriminated against in heterosexual society. The attitudes are the same. As it turns out, the best thing to be, straight or gay, is a man. Still, Charlotte insists that she wouldn't dress like a man for anything—not even for love. Wearing, say, a man's suit would constitute a betrayal of herself, would in fact feel like drag in a way that wearing a dress does not.

If "drag queen" is a term that seems inappropriate where Charlotte is concerned, it may be because the frivolous, good-time connotations are so much at odds with her grave domesticity; she calls herself a transvestite—a label that, ironically, drag queens in Amsterdam or London or New York reject as being too serious and clinical. Let the party girls go out on the town. Charlotte's vanity takes a different form: she is house-proud, not exhibitionistic.

"I have always dressed simply," she maintains. It is said that she takes after her mother, who never wore makeup either. In her *Hausfrau* drag, Charlotte makes her way through her museum, winding the clocks, polishing the wood until it shines, turning the lights off behind her. Like many women of her age, she has her memories. "At times the men really ran after me," she confides to the camera in von Praunheim's movie. "One doesn't bloom in vain."

....

Marlene Dietrich, who died in 1991, is buried in Berlin's Friedenau cemetery. In Babelsberg, a western suburb, the DEFA studios still stand. It is there that Josef von Sternberg made *The Blue Angel*, the now-classic movie that launched Dietrich's career, and there that Charlotte von Mahlsdorf has provided furniture and objects from her museum as props for period films. It is there that Charlotte has worked as an actress on occasion, playing bit parts (in Horst Seemann's *Beethoven—Tage aus einem Leben*, or *Beethoven—A Day in the Life*, she appeared in two roles, as a master violin maker and as a woman at a ball).

Dietrich's apotheosis as a drag goddess took place during her lifetime, and the fascination shows no signs of abating. Strapsharry continues to immortalize her in his nightclub act. Other cabarets, geared to the tourists' expectations, routinely feature one or two numbers by a drag queen with high-arched eyebrows and a smoky voice—not so much a direct tribute to Dietrich herself as to the drag queens of the thirties, who paid tribute to her as their contemporary. Meanwhile, in New York, a new generation of followers convene for the "Night of a Thousand Marlenes," all of them dressing to emulate their idol. That these are men celebrating a woman who dared to dress as a man is a paradox that goes unremarked.

Dietrich's obituary in the *International Herald Tribune* quoted her definition of glamour, which might serve as a manifesto of sorts for her drag followers. "Glamour is assurance," she said. "It is a kind of knowing that you are all right in every way, mentally and physically and in appearance, and that, whatever the occasion or the situation, you are equal to it."

Among Ichgola Androgyn's most prized possessions is a pair of Marlene Dietrich's false eyelashes.

AMBITION

He was surprised, though he knew they were men, how much they looked like women. Beautiful women. He had never in his life seen women look more beautiful or feminine than the queens strolling about the floor of the ballroom.

HUGH SELBY, "STRIKE,"
Last Exit to Brooklyn

....

The stores in the Siam Center, a concrete-and-glass shopping mall that is Bangkok's temple of high fashion, sell the genuine article and the knockoff, side by side. The authentic Jean Paul Gaultier jacket, bought as a prototype, hangs with the reproductions that sell for a fraction of its price. Out on the streets, vendors hawk "Lacoste" polo shirts, "Christian Dior" perfumes, and "Rolex" watches. There is nothing tongue-in-cheek or playfully fake about these copies; they are in dead earnest, intended to stand in for the originals. "Gucci" bags come complete with the "Made In Italy" legend. The latest releases by Bruce Springsteen and U2 blare from cassette decks at booths that deal in pirated tapes. In the bars, the drag queens are every bit as believable, the fake women indistinguishable from the real.

On a steamy night in May, the bars that line Patpong 2, at the heart of Bangkok's red-light district, are doing a listless business. Some feature boxing rings and pool tables; many are open to the sidewalks, where the touts chase down foreign tourists as the wholesome sound of Amy Grant singing "Baby, Baby, Baby" spills out into the street. At the Limelight, to the accompaniment of fifteen-year-old hit songs by Creedence Clearwater Revival, young women writhe absentmindedly on an elevated dance floor. They eye the customers: two men reading aloud from a guidebook, in German; three Japanese, drinking champagne; a sullen-looking American in a flowered shirt, sitting alone. From her post at the end of a banquette upholstered in gray velveteen, the *mamasan*—a sort of den mother who, here as in many bars in Bangkok, is in fact a matronly, middle-aged drag queen—boasts that the girls' makeup is her doing: she has taught them how to apply eye shadow, how to shape their eyebrows, how to outline their lips before filling in the color. The columns are paved with mirrors reflecting the green neon tubing, the flashing lights, and the girls seen from all angles, dressed in bikinis and high heels. One tugs from time to time at the seat of her bathing suit, which rides up as she dances. Each girl wears a badge with a number on it, to be sure that there is no confusion when the customer makes his selection.

Number 21 is a *katoey*, or "lady-boy"—the Thai term for drag queen—according to one of the bar girls, who confides this information and then instantly retracts it for fear that she will be punished by the management. "Is the lady-boy a transsexual?" I persist, but the bar girl moves away and goes to sit with the Germans, persuading them to buy her an orange juice (alcohol being a man's prerogative in Thailand). She looks shy and slightly ill at ease, as the three of them attempt conversation—she, nearly naked, and they, fully clothed. The bikinis that are the girls' uniform are peculiar to the bars here, since Thai women cover up when they go to the beach, showing as little bare skin as possible; some wear their clothing into the water. Like the girls, the lady-boy wears a bikini, but, unlike them, she wears it with pride.

Compared with Japanese women, Tanizaki said, Western women are better seen from a distance. So are Western drag queens, it would seem, after comparison with Bangkok's lady-boys. Thai men have smaller builds, smaller features, smaller hands and feet, and smoother skin, with less body hair. The illusion is intact, even at close range. The visitor is easily fooled.

So easily, in fact, that some transvestites in Bangkok turn to crime, confident that their disguise is infallible. In 1991, local law enforcement officials added transvestites to the watch list of potential troublemakers drawn up in advance of the World Bank and International Monetary Fund conference, and the Bangkok police began a file of nude photographs of hundreds of transvestites and transsexuals—a measure denounced by the *Bangkok Post* as "an affront to human rights and dignity." Lt. Col. Kachornsak Kraingsakchit of the Tourist Police, however, defended the initiative, claiming that not only were most of the victims incapable of identifying their attackers, they didn't even know whether they'd been attacked by a man or a woman. "I don't blame them," Lieutenant Colonel Kachornsak said, "because some [transvestites] are actually even more beautiful and sexier than real bar girls." The following year, in a highly publicized case, four transvestites (one, a transsexual) robbed a Hong Kong businessman and others by first inducing their victims to suck on their nipples, which had been coated with a tranquilizer.

Whether or not Bangkok's drag queens are indeed the criminals they are often suspected of being, their ability to transform themselves so convincingly arouses fear and mistrust, as well as fascination. In many cases, the *appearance* of a woman is beyond reproach, and the only giveaway—the only clue to the gender of the body beneath the clothes—is the behavior. For instance, Thai culture forbids women to expose their breasts in public; lady-boys, however, feel no compunctions about showing off their implants or a bustline acquired by taking birth control pills. So, paradoxically, the sight of what might otherwise, elsewhere, be the sure sign of a real woman is in Thailand the telltale sign of a man.

At the Love Boat, down the street from the Limelight, I turn to the Thai friend acting as my guide and wonder aloud, "Is that a woman or a lady-boy?" The object of our attention is dressed in a black halter dress, studded with rhinestones, and high heels. She is dancing with a sandy-haired man in a "Levi's 501" T-shirt, hanging on him, her arms around his neck.

"That's a lady-boy," the friend says.

"How can you tell?" I ask.

"This one is easy," the friend replies. "No Thai woman—not even a prostitute—would dance in public with her arms around a man's neck."

For all that they may look exactly like women, lady-boys are often characterized by an unladylike lack of inhibition—a careless spontaneity that has as its base a sense of entitlement, which in Thai society women are denied. At a bar called Harrie's, on Patpong 3, a lady-boy who goes by the name of Natasha claims that she studies women all the time—their posture, their gestures. Often, she says, she ends up feeling sorry for them and wanting to help them, to give them a few pointers on how to be more attractive, more feminine. Sometimes, though, she sees a woman do something she likes, something she can use, and then she appropriates it for herself; it becomes a part of her repertoire. Natasha's every move seems not studied, exactly, but not spontaneous, either—like choreography in a dance routine learned years ago and performed daily ever since, until it became rote. She sits with her torso twisted, her shoulders turned in opposition to her hips, her legs crossed. Her hands flutter from time to time, adding grace notes to her conversation, then return to rest quietly in her lap. She tucks her chin, demurely, and looks up at her listener from behind a side-parted curtain of long, straight hair. She has accurately mastered these attitudes, on a perfectly plausible scale. Still, it is hard to shake the awareness that they are acquired, that Natasha's demeanor is some sort of overlay, and one senses that at any moment she might revert to a manner that is bolder and more forthright, should the occasion call for it.

Like the lady-boys, the girls who work the bars in Patpong are accused of being more assertive than Thai women are supposed to be. Their body language is similarly Western and suggestive, copied from movies and fashion magazines. But while the lady-boys exude an air of rigorous control, of aggression held in check, the bar girls' recklessness seems fitful and uneasy. The reticence that the lady-boys strive so hard to emulate requires no special effort on the girls' part; like most daughters, they were indoctrinated early on with the conditions of femininity. Somewhere between male aggression and female passivity lies a no-man's-land where the lady-boys and the bar girls meet, having come to it from opposite directions.

Any consideration of Bangkok's lady-boys must take the bar girls into account as well. More often than not, they share the same goals: a decent income, a way out. In Patpong, they are often thrown together, patrolling the same small turf and competing for the same clients. They are also bound by the same collective fantasies—salable notions of an idealized femininity, comprehensible at first glance. Even government-sponsored programs in occupational retraining lump male transvestite prostitutes and female prostitutes together, in a curriculum that includes lessons in hairdressing, dressmaking, and jewelry-making.

Thailand's rampant poverty and its permissive morals have conspired to make it fertile ground for prostitution; salaries for unskilled labor are nowhere near the money to be made in the bars. Prostitution is widely available and relatively free of the stigma that attaches to it in the West. One recent survey estimated that three-fourths of all sexually active Thai men frequent brothels or massage parlors (or maintain some other extramarital relations), and that the vast majority of young Thai males have their first sexual experience with a prostitute.

In her book *Patpong Sisters: An American Woman's View of the Bangkok Sex World*, Cleo Odzer writes of a little girl in a remote village in the northeast who told her schoolteacher, "You look as pretty as a whore today." Many Thai prostitutes from the provinces send money to their families, providing them with luxuries the neighbors can't afford. On trips back home, the prostitutes are treated like local celebrities. Skilled in the art of makeup, wearing fashionable clothes, they are the most glamorous creatures many small-town inhabitants have ever seen, belying (or so it seems) the grisly stories of child prostitution and of women unable to escape when their brothel catches fire because their pimp has chained them to their beds. Attitudes toward the value of female children in rural areas of Thailand have undergone a change, owing in large part to the earning power of prostitutes. In an article in 1993, Lillian S. Robinson, a writer for *The Nation* (one of Bangkok's two English-language daily newspapers), quoted Thanh-Dam Truong, a sociologist: "As a result of new opportunities to sell a daughter into prostitution, female sexual capacity is perceived as having a market value taking 'predominance over male labour. . . . Families actually celebrate the birth of a daughter, because she now has potentially more access to social mobility.' "

Early one evening, before getting down to business, two lady-boys who work the streets of Patpong on a "freelance" basis sit at Dunkin' Donuts discussing their profession and their goals. Both are in their early twenties. One, by the name of Meong, got her start as a go-go boy at a gay bar on Patpong 3. The main factor in her decision to start working in drag, she says matter-of-factly, was financial: the rates for girls are generally higher. There is no shame in dressing in drag here, she and her friend insist. During the seventies, the Thai minister of defense won the national contest for best female dresser. More recently, one popular TV sitcom featured a cast of lady-boys.

Her friend, who calls herself "Cherrie," pulls from her purse a picture of Demi Moore, torn from the pages of a two-year-old issue of *People* magazine; she's been told that she looks like the actress, she says. The resemblance is vague but not far-fetched and not something she seems to cultivate—her hair is cut in a different style, for one thing. Thai drag queens may portray famous women when they're performing in a revue, but offstage they play themselves. Cherrie contends that it's important for a woman to be beautiful because people like to look at beauty, and it's a woman's job to be pleasing. Meong nods in agreement. They both like what they call "boutique clothes" and cite Pierre Balmain, Pierre Cardin, Yves Saint Laurent, and Chanel as their favorite labels. Neither of them, however, could be accused of such high chic tonight. Cherrie is wearing bronze leather hot pants, a black ribbed tank top, high-heeled sandals, and mauve nail polish; Meong is dressed in a crocheted cotton sweater, a polka-dot miniskirt, and open-toed slingbacks. Every once in a while, Meong says, they find a customer willing to take them shopping—some *farang*, or foreigner, who follows them on a tour of the stores in the Siam Center, footing the bill with his credit card. Asked whether there is such a thing as bad drag, and if so, what it is, Meong and Cherrie need no time to ponder the question. Bad drag, they reply, is clothes that are not up-to-date.

Throughout Patpong, stories about the bar girl or the lady-boy who found a rich client to marry her and take her away from it all make the rounds on a regular basis. In some versions, the lady-boy has had a sex change and the unsuspecting husband (who is often German) has set her up in palatial splendor somewhere in Europe (usually Switzerland). In others, the girl or lady-boy is swept off to a career as a high-paid fashion model in the West. The moral of the story is always the same: by exploiting their beauty, women—or men who present themselves as women—can escape their circumstances.

The song playing at the King's Paradise is "One Night in Bangkok," which (along with *The King and I* and a documentary about the local AIDS epidemic) has been banned by Thai authorities. A lady-boy in a pinstripe skirt watches a group of Westerners playing pool at the table in the corner. Men cluster around the black-linoleum bar, their arms draped over the naked shoulders of smiling women. The music changes: "I'll give you television, I'll give you eyes of blue," David Bowie sings. At 2:15 A.M., the ropes around the boxing ring are removed, and it becomes the stage for the nightly drag show. A chorus of seven enters, wearing tucked bodices, stoles, headdresses, and sarong skirts—all made from gold lamé that has been (ingeniously) draped and tied rather than sewn. Some of the performers have breasts; some are wearing hairpieces. The lip-synching is highly approximate. The choreography is rudimentary, consisting primarily of walking and arm-waving, in unison. In the audience, a lady-boy wearing a stretch minidress pulls a compact out of her fake Chanel bag and retouches her white lipstick outlined in black.

Two regulars rate the drag shows at various clubs around town. The most famous, at the Calypso, is strictly for tourists, in their opinion—an elaborate production usually based on a hackneyed theme, like Berlin in the thirties. At Rome, the cast is pretty much the same, though the repertory leans more toward Shirley Bassey, Donna Summer, and Diana Ross, the standard icons. At Manuel, the entertainment is a live rendition of the latest video clips from England and America, including Madonna's *Open Your Heart*, in which she dances in a man's suit, shoes, and hat. Here, it's performed by a lady-boy who has copied all her moves, as well as her costume, adding yet another layer of ambiguity: a man dressed as a woman playing at dressing like a man. But the regulars prefer this show, at the King's Paradise. It's less commercial, they insist, not so slick. For the next number—a song made famous by Teresa Teng, a Chinese pop star with a huge following in Asia—a chubby chanteuse in a white sequined mermaid dress steps into the spotlight; she is wearing temple bells as earrings.

By day, Patpong is still a business district. The buildings are low, dwarfed by the skyscrapers that have sprung up around them. Patpong 1 and 2, parallel cross streets, connect Silom Road and Surawong Road, both busy thoroughfares. At night, Patpong 1 is closed to traffic. Patpong 3, a nearby impasse, specializes in gay bars. The streets and the immediate neighborhood belong to Udom Patpong, a Thai of Chinese descent, educated in America and, in England, at the

London School of Economics. In 1946, he persuaded his father to cut a road through what had been a banana plantation with a teak house in the middle. His earliest tenants were airlines, news services, restaurants, and one massage parlor. By 1966, there were seven bars. Then the boom began. Descriptions of Patpong in the late sixties, when U.S. soldiers in the Vietnam War came to Bangkok for their R&R, depict the streets crawling with GIs and—in what amounts to a kind of intramural drag—Thai girls imitating the American girls back home, dressed in miniskirts, fishnet stockings, and go-go boots despite the hundred-degree heat.

Since the full-scale withdrawal of American military forces from Southeast Asia, in 1976, Thailand's prostitution industry has been sustained by tourism and an image of Bangkok as a hedonist's paradise, where every whim is indulged, albeit for a price. When, in 1990, Rudolf Pieper, a nightclub entrepreneur who had had a hand in Danceteria, the Palladium, and the Tunnel in New York, opened a new venture called Mars BKK in Patpong, he told *The New York Times:* "People come from all over looking for this let-go atmosphere they can't find at home in the West." In the *Bangkok Post,* Bernard Trink, an American journalist, has written a popular column on local nightlife since 1966, reviewing Patpong's bars—the service, the food, the drinks, the girls—for the benefit of English-speaking foreign men, singling out the women who are especially adept at pleasing their clients and, like a proud connoisseur, telling his readers where to find them.

At any given moment, the bars in Patpong now number nearly one hundred, with the names changing so quickly that the guidebooks are out-of-date before they are printed. "I never really intended to bring in the bars, it just happened," Udom Patpong told a reporter from the *Independent* in 1991. "It was fun during my younger days, going around and talking to the bar owners." Mr. Patpong oversees his real estate empire, with the help of his two sisters, from a cramped fifth-floor office in the thick of the action. Perhaps because he continues to charge rents that are among the lowest in central Bangkok, the streets that bear his name are nowhere to be found on the Thai version of the Monopoly board, although Silom Road is. "We could have made a lot more money, but what for?" he said. "We have no other business to invest in." He has consistently turned down offers from developers who would raze the bars to make way for office buildings, because, he claims, he has long-standing relationships with the barkeepers, and he refuses to throw them out.

....

In a gay bar on Patpong 3, up a steep flight of stairs, the *mamasan*— a lady-boy of a certain age—greets customers from behind the bar, her portly form wrapped in a frowsy-looking dressing gown. The room is long and narrow, with young Thai men in kimonos worn open over G-strings circulating among the customers, who sit, fully dressed, laughing at one another's lewd jokes and taking stock of the well-built staff. This bar is engaged in what one *farang*, an Australian expatriate who frequents the place, refers to as "strictly a takeout business." The employees here are straight, he insists, and they take these jobs as a matter of expediency. One nineteen-year-old confirms this: he works as a go-go boy, he explains, to support his wife and infant son. In Thailand, the expatriate continues, sexuality is not regarded as the foundation of a person's identity, as it is in the West. Bisexuality is fairly commonplace, and homosexuality unexceptional.

In Buddhism as it is construed here, being born a woman is the consequence of one's bad deeds in a former life. Karma determines not only social status, wealth, and power but also gender. Thai superstition warns against women defiling men: a man whose clothes are washed along with a woman's, or a man who passes by an area where a woman's clothes are hung to dry, may lose his sexual potency. Money is regarded as an evil, and female nature as materialistic. The spiritual domain is masculine, and the path to enlightenment is for men, not for women. The most that a woman can hope for is to perform enough good deeds in this life that she will be reincarnated as a man in the next.

In every society in which the power resides with men, the act of a man dressing as a woman constitutes a radical political gesture—a deliberate abdication of the privileges that are his birthright, a willful identification with his inferiors. In Thailand, drag's subversive aspect is even more pronounced than it is in many other countries. Women's rights—many of them self-evident elsewhere, such as a woman's right to apply for a passport without her husband's permission—are astonishingly recent here, and there is no feminist movement to speak of. It is only since 1935, in an attempt to cast itself as a modern nation hospitable to Western ethics, that Thailand established monogamy as the legal grounds for marriage, and only since 1976 that a woman can be granted a divorce on the basis of her husband's adultery. Even so, without any provisions for enforcing the monogamy law, the practice of polygyny continues, particularly in the upper class, in the long-standing custom of the minor wife, or *mia noy*—a sort of institutionalized mistress.

At eight-thirty, at Kentucky Fried Chicken, a lady-boy who goes by the name of Gigi comes in for a soda and sits at one of the tables overlooking Silom Road. Even in this harsh fluorescent lighting, she looks utterly believable, in a black lace bodysuit, a zip-front black patent leather dress, and boots to match. She is twenty now, she says, and has been doing drag since she was eight, in the beginning wearing whatever she could borrow. These days she is employed as a hairdresser at the Central Department Store, where she wears a uniform to work. She is crazy about fashion, she says, and she likes foreign fashion designers, because their ideas tend to be "fancier"; her favorite is Thierry Mugler. She loves to put on something sexy and go to a club, where men approach her. The conversation turns to karma. Given the perfection of her feminine image, would she like to come back in the next life as a woman? Absolutely not, she replies. A woman's life would not be challenging the way a drag queen's life is. Next time, she says, she hopes to be reincarnated—again—as a drag queen. This is fun, she insists. This life is the best.

To the extent that Thai women are affected by changing attitudes toward women elsewhere, the lady-boys are, too. In her book *Providence and Prostitution: Image and Reality for Women in Buddhist Thailand*, Khin Thitsa writes of the image Thai women have been assigned by men abroad—an image that the bar girls and the lady-boys alike do their best to live up to. "It would seem that the women's liberation movement, increasingly active in the developed countries, has this one unfortunate consequence for women of the Third World countries: their men, perhaps on the surface adjusting to new demands for respect from their countrywomen, come to Thailand and the Philippines to exploit exotic Eastern flowers. The travel advertisements themselves, often in sex magazines, hint to the men 'that they will live like kings in Bangkok with the most beautiful women of the East by their side. . . . The man who has difficulty establishing relationships . . . in Bangkok can choose among hundreds of young women who, for a tiny amount, will make him feel like a great Don Juan.' "

If a woman's task is to instill in a man a sense of his own importance, then the prevailing femininity is timid and accommodating. The woman is small, the better to make a man feel huge. She is passive, the better to make him feel powerful. She is attentive, in order to make him feel fascinating. "The first thing you learn after fellatio is how to listen," Lillian S. Robinson wrote in her survey of prostitutes in Bangkok.

Part of the acknowledged appeal of these transactions in Bangkok is that they are blurred, not strictly business. Cleo Odzer delineates the circumstances:

> Unlike prostitution in the West, the encounter between the Thai bar girl and the *farang* may not have the cultural appearance of a deal. At first the girl establishes rapport, staging attraction and praising the man. Then she offers to spend the night without mentioning a price. She leaves the amount up to him so that the money has the appearance of a gift. When she stays with him for a period of time, the money she asks for is not represented as payment but as reimbursement for the money she's lost from the bar and/or support for her family. The *farang* can't tell if she's really in love with him or is only after cash. . . . The men who fall in love with bar girls are entrenched in the ambiguity of never being sure if the women are girlfriends or whores.

Many lady-boys report that their conduct is along the same lines, in their attempts to flatter men and in the hope of finding one who will set them up in a new life. *Katoey*, or lady-boy, in Thai is a label used not only for drag queens but for transsexuals and effeminate gay men as well. The *katoey*'s opposite is the "complete male," and while the lady-boy's role is to remain passive and submissive during sex, the "complete male" is defined as "the penetrating man." If lady-boys employ all sorts of elaborate strategies in bed, in the dark, for deceiving their customers as to their true gender, most agree that they succeed primarily because their customers *want* to be deceived: having been attracted by the signals of a woman, they want to believe that they are making love to a woman. Most lady-boys in Patpong claim that their customers are heterosexual men who find the idea of sex with a man repellent.

Not all Bangkok's lady-boys set out to look like bombshells. At the coffee shop at Robinson's department store, the waiters—waitresses?—all sport the same androgynous uniform: a tattersall-checked blouse, pleated trousers, and mid-heel pumps. Their hair is cut in the same pageboy style. They wear earrings but no makeup. The monitor mounted high on a wall in the corner is tuned to MTV: Prince's "Money Doesn't Matter" is blaring in the background, covered intermittently by the din of clattering dishes. Juggling plates, the staff moves among tables draped with black-and-white Op Art–patterned oilcloth. The customers, most of them office workers on their lunch breaks, seem oblivious to the obvious: Are these waiters women, so secure in their femininity that they don't feel obliged to endear themselves to the world by means of the customary signals? Or are they men, so confident in their ability to present themselves as women that they shun the usual trappings as too blatant and predictable? Their gestures are undeniably feminine—graceful, soft, demure, contradicted only by a certain brusque efficiency and an aloofness surprising in a country where the service is consistently ingratiating. It is their voices that betray them, as their hushed falsetto grows preposterously shrill in an effort to be heard over the music.

It's eleven o'clock on a Sunday night, May 1992. At the King's Lounge, an upstairs bar (next door to the King's Corner and not far from the King's Paradise), the lady-boys are lounging around like a pack of sorority girls in a dormitory, waiting for the party to start. The scene doesn't reach its peak until sometime after two, when many people making the rounds of the bars stop by at the end of the night. For now, there are only a few stragglers. Video monitors positioned behind the bar and at intervals around the room's perimeter alternate between music videos, for dancing, and the local Channel 7 coverage of the Miss Universe pageant, held in Bangkok the night before, at the

Queen Sirikit National Convention Center. The dance floor is empty, but the lady-boys, seated on their barstools, bounce in time to a Salt-N-Pepa song. "Ladies? All the ladies," Salt-N-Pepa sing; "Louder now—help me out, come on! All the ladies!"

The lady-boys join in and shout the refrain: "Let's talk about sex!"

A friend—this one a *farang*—returning from the men's room recites some of the graffiti on the walls there for my benefit: "You can take the girl out of the bar but you can't take the bar out of the girl."

Coverage of the Miss Universe pageant has progressed to the evening-gown competition. The lady-boys gather round the monitors for a closer look.

Miss Nicaragua wears a gown with concentric circles of silver sequins—like targets—over her breasts. The lady-boys elbow one another in the ribs.

Miss Costa Rica, in a pink gown with a high quilted collar and a train, smiles earnestly for the camera. The lady-boys shake their heads.

They cheer at the appearance of Miss U.S.A., a blonde in a long black chemise so narrow that she has trouble walking; when she totters for a moment, descending the stairs, a little collective sigh of sympathy goes up.

Miss Colombia's necklace—an asymmetrical affair that looks like a rhinestone boa constrictor coiled lazily around her neck—inspires a moment's quizzical silence, then a rapid exchange of opinions. With her hair wound into a high French twist, her dark red lipstick, her strapless gown, she has clearly made a concerted effort to be glamorous—a fact that is not lost on the lady-boy audience.

Miss Venezuela comes in for criticism on her makeup, which—it's agreed—lacks subtlety.

Miss Belgium, however, gets a round of applause. A blonde in the Goldie Hawn tradition, she looks as if she'd been poured into a green sequined strapless dress with a pointed bodice; she wears long gloves to match.

The lady-boys pick their favorite candidates as the judges tally their scores.

And then the six finalists are announced. Miss Belgium, for one. Unanimous approval, cheers all around. Miss Venezuela, with her heavy-handed makeup and her frozen smile. Bewilderment. Miss Colombia, with her snakelike necklace. Controversy. With a mixture of awe, fascination, and skepticism, the lady-boys stare at the final lineup—at the dresses slit to the thigh, the hairdos, the walks. "Is it just my imagination," my friend asks as we sit there in their midst, his gaze fixed on one of the monitors, "or do these beauty contestants look like drag queens?"

ALLURE

For women are not (judging by my own short experience of the sex) obedient, chaste, scented, and exquisitely apparelled by nature. They can only attain these graces, without which they may enjoy none of the delights of life, by the most tedious discipline.

VIRGINIA WOOLF,
Orlando

The woman who comes by her beauty naturally is not necessarily intelligent or clever or even congenial—just lucky. The credit rightfully goes not to her but to her Maker. Sheer physical beauty is omnipotent, of course, and if you are blessed with it, it may inspire strangers to carry your suitcases and heartsick men to write long-winded poems in your honor, but the fact is that in the final analysis—in drag queens as in women—beauty is not terribly *interesting*, in and of itself. That, at any rate, is Lola's conviction. Of all the drag queens on the club scene in Paris, she has the reputation for being the most consistently, indisputably chic. Lola has been to New York, where she saw drag queens gotten up to look like supermodels. They were dressed in simple clothes, not unlike the ones that Linda Evangelista and Naomi Campbell wear—Azzedine Alaïa–style stretch dresses, cut very short and skintight, to show off their bodies. Like the supermodels themselves, the drag queens who portray them have, genetically speaking, won the lottery. For Lola, however, they have taken the easy way out.

Mind you, Lola isn't *un*attractive. She has even features and delicate bones. But as with any woman who turns to fashion as a means for presenting herself to her best advantage, Lola has cultivated a distinct personal style. She carries herself with authority, as if a spotlight followed her around. She dresses with sophistication and wit. Heads turn.

Born and raised near Lausanne, in Switzerland, Lola came to Paris to study fashion at the age of eighteen, in 1983. After graduation, she stayed on, taking a job as an assistant to Jean Paul Gaultier, in his design studio. More recently, Lola has been working on a freelance basis, as a designer and stylist. She has served as a consultant to Escada, the German label, offering advice on the clothing line and overseeing the accessories. She orchestrates photo shoots, conceptualizing the picture and selecting the outfits, down to the last detail. Dressed in drag (which she does only in the evenings, for parties or for going out to clubs), she likes to think of herself as a "couture queen," a paragon of high fashion. She makes her own clothes—sketching the idea, mapping the pattern, cutting the fabric, sewing them herself, in the painstaking tradition she learned during an apprenticeship in the haute couture ateliers at the house of di Marino, which produced the designs of Yves Saint Laurent, Givenchy, and Christian Lacroix, in Lausanne.

Drag is for Lola an extension of designing, a way of putting her ideas into practice. Sometimes, she says, she wants to see what something looks like when it's worn. "I think that when one designs clothes," she explains, "one has somewhere, to some extent, the fantasy of wearing them. For me, it's no longer a fantasy, because I wear the dress in fact. It's not only the dress that I like; it's the whole look— the makeup, the hairstyle, the bag, the shoes that go with it." Fashion in former times was "a constraint," Lola acknowledges: "the high heels, the boned corsets, the obligation to hold yourself rigid all the time, to carry your handbag and your umbrella, to wear a hat." If women no longer go to all that trouble, Lola doesn't blame them. Still, she says, it would be a shame if a certain fastidious attention to detail were to die out altogether. So she comes to its rescue on a fairly steady basis, keeping it alive for a limited audience.

Lola changes her hair color according to the look she's trying to achieve. Hairdresser friends lend her wigs and style them for her. Other friends, who work as makeup artists, help her to create a face in keeping with the image of the clothes. She finds shoes at the annual Hermès sale, and other accessories through the network of her professional contacts at designers' and manufacturers' showrooms. In fact, she says, she buys very little, being handy with a needle and thread.

Despite the fact that many of her friends dress in the style of the late seventies, of Yves Saint Laurent's heyday—in trousers, shoes with a high, chunky heel, a belted blazer—Lola says that her favorite period, hands down, is the fifties. A scholar of fashion history, she admires Balenciaga, Charles James, Christian Dior, as well as Hollywood stars like Jayne Mansfield, Marilyn Monroe, Ava Gardner. Lola looks back to the fifties as "a more womanly time," she says. Fashion models in those days were "already women"—thirty-five years old in some instances, whereas today they're teenagers. To her mind, Bettina, a model who figured prominently in the pages of fifties fashion magazines, is a bigger star than Linda or Naomi will ever be.

For *The Face*, the English magazine, Lola has collaborated with Pierre and Gilles, two French photographers who work as a team. There she is, occupying a full page, wearing a marabou-trimmed pink-sequined peignoir: an ersatz Hollywood goddess in her Technicolor boudoir furnished with a crystal chandelier and a fluffy, stuffed white lapdog. On other occasions, Lola has transformed herself into an exact, human replica of a Barbie doll, sporting a Barbie-style wardrobe.

In French, someone who dresses in drag is said to be *"en travesti"* (translated as "in disguise"), a relatively neutral term, for all its intimations of parody—a term that, as it made its way into English, lost its connotations of transvestism and acquired a broader meaning predicated on gross exaggeration, which the word *travesty* not only recognizes but also deplores. Lola contends that drag is not a faithful reproduction of femininity but in certain respects, she says in English, "a travesty of it." Drag in her case, she contends, has nothing to do with wanting to be a woman, or with wanting to become a woman, or even with wanting to look like a woman. It's a matter of wanting to be the belle of the ball, Queen for a Day, the center of attention. While other drag queens may dress as a provocation, or an act of aggression, Lola claims that she has no need to vindicate herself, no scores to settle. "I just want to be looked at," she insists. "That's all. I want people to notice me and look at me really closely. Because it's different being looked at as a woman and being looked at as a man.

"I think every human being contains the capacity to be both sexes.

It's something that occupies more or less importance in different people's lives. I have a personality that's rather androgynous. There are some moments when I feel more feminine and other times when I feel more masculine. And it's difficult to manage the two, when one has always the same appearance. It's a little like having a double personality—even the comportment is different. In the end, dressing in drag permits me to live out both of them."

Lola makes the distinction between the drag queens who dress up "just for fun" and the full-time types, many of whom work the shows in the bars in Pigalle, playing song-and-dance acts to tourists from the provinces. The latter kind doesn't interest her; she is one of the former, of which, she concedes, there are only a few in Paris. She considers herself part of the new generation of drag queens who came of age in the wake of the eighties fashion frenzy, a kind of widespread hysteria about clothes. Now that people are dressing in a more sober manner—"simple," according to Lola's descriptions, "and rather strict"—there are those who find it frustrating, who long for an outlet for their imaginations, who are looking to be, in her words, "a bit more spirited." Drag provides them with that opportunity. If there's a resurgence of drag these days, Lola contends, it's because everything is running counter to it: times are "harder and more serious," politics "more repressive." And so, she says, "there is much more irreverence at night." She agrees that AIDS has played a part, encouraging a kind of exhibitionism that is an end in itself. "There's a saying," she adds: *"le corps, a défaut de se donner, se montre"*—the body, if it can't put out, puts itself on display.

The display of the body being the business of fashion, Lola follows the work of many designers with interest. She is a fan of Thierry Mugler, who has what she calls "a delirious imagination." Dominatrixes, Valkyries, intergalactic biker chicks, diabolical Barbie dolls, Las Vegas showgirls—they are all part of the cast of ongoing characters in his repertory. His severe suits, his corset tops, his set-piece evening costumes are flattering, Lola finds, whether they're for a drag queen or for a woman. For his runway shows, Mugler has routinely sent out drag queens as models, and more often than not they are indistinguishable from the genuine women—their waists cinched, the clothes boned to coax the body into the shape that femininity takes in our minds.

But for the most part, Lola admires not so much entire collections or particular designers as an outfit here, an idea there. She has, she says, "a horror of the haute couture." Despite her fondness for its tradition, her respect for the "sensitivity" and "refinement" that go into making a garment by hand, she finds the clothes ugly, lacking all inspiration, expensive-looking—bogged down in beading and embroidery, with no thought for the silhouette, the image overall. Perhaps, she wonders, it's a matter of the couturier catering to the clients, most of whom Lola finds sadly lacking in the taste department. Whether the designer has put his own vision in the service of the workmanship, or whether he has curtailed his imagination to suit the women who buy the most, to Lola's mind he has defaulted on his sacred responsibility. It is up to fashion designers to set the highest standards that women at any particular moment aspire to, and so, Lola says, it's no wonder that women today are at such a loss.

"La femme est naturelle, c'est-à-dire abominable," Baudelaire wrote. Woman is natural—which is to say, abominable. A recent ad campaign for Weill lingerie, posted on bus shelters and signs all over Paris, proclaimed *"L'art d'être une femme."* The art of being a woman. The subjugation of nature—making order of its chaos, regulating its vagaries, superimposing on it some grand, man-made design—is to the French way of thinking a noble endeavor, undertaken no less fervently where human nature is concerned. Like animals and plants, people need to be domesticated in order to live in harmony. If artifice is the essence of civilization, then femininity—an elaborate code of appearance and behavior by which ordinary women are transformed into delectable confections—is surely among its crowning achievements. Femininity is in this context a higher, more refined degree of womanhood, a collectively agreed-upon representation taken for granted to such an extent that it becomes synonymous with womanhood itself. A model wearing high heels, lipstick, perfume, and a dress that accentuates her bustline and her hips is an *idea* of a woman, just as trees planted in soldierly rows and cascades engineered to fall at carefully measured intervals are an idea of nature. That women manage to transform themselves into convincing replicas of this idea is remarkable enough, in and of itself; that Lola does, too, is in some respects an even greater accomplishment.

She invokes the little tricks that by this time belong to feminine lore, passed down from one generation of women to the next, from fashion magazines to their readers: a visual sleight-of-hand that can minimize so-called figure problems and emphasize a woman's best features, helping her to present an idealized version of herself. The notion of copying clothes from photographs or other sources is anathema to Lola, not only because it smacks of a lack of creativity but also because she might run the risk of looking like someone else—if not the woman in the picture, then another drag queen who had settled on the same inspiration. Lola knows that many drag queens in America and elsewhere imitate Marilyn Monroe and Liza Minnelli and Madonna, and that in those instances verisimilitude becomes the standard by which success is measured. But Lola reserves her highest respect for the drag queen—and the woman—who is a true original. At the Folies Pigalle, where she and her friends often go on Saturday nights, or at the Kit-Kat, where they congregate afterward, the best *travelos*, or drag queens, are the ones with their own personal style. Every woman who, having missed out on beauty at birth, spent her adolescence poring over fashion magazines—studying the science of self-presentation, acquiring the skills that would enable her to command attention in her own right—will find a heroine in Lola. She represents the triumph of elegance over beauty, of sophistication and refinement over the luck of the draw.

The sound of steady rain in the courtyard. A damp chill that finds its way through three layers of clothes into the bones. There is not a taxi to be had in all of Paris. All over the city, people are turning on their Minitels.

An electronic monitor and keyboard hooked up to an ordinary `telephone, the Minitel gives the lovelorn access to astrological advice (call 3615 and type AIDEZMOI, MONDESTIN, or any of the other services' code words); the tired or the lazy, to home-delivered dinners; the insomniac businessman, to his bank balance; the bored, to games (3615 JEUBRIDGE or 3615 SCRABBLE); the stranded—theoretically—to a taxi. The on-line dating services, of which there are some two thousand five hundred (with code names like FUSION, MATRIMO, and ONLYYOU)— some gay, some explicitly sexual, some geared expressly to marriage—

initially prompted a raft of speculation in the press about what would become of a society in which young professionals resorted to their Minitels for love, but the concern seems to have subsided. Now a standard fixture in the domestic landscape, the Minitel has brought the inhabitants of some six and a half million French homes and offices into the electronic era—a future that evidently welcomes everyone. On this particular evening, when the only response to repeated requests for a cab on 3615 TAXIS BLEUS is the same refrain—"Nothing at the moment, please call us back"—the *travelos* of Paris are staying home, congregating by means of the Minitel (3615 TRAV).

From the top of a blank black screen, white lines appear, filling in the shape of a blond wig parted on the side, then the eyes, then a sexy mouth, a necklace, a close-fitting bodice with heart-shaped breasts, a boa: here is the electronic hostess. She winks. Please type in your pseudonym. The main menu appears on the screen, a choice of twelve possible options, among them, "DIALOGUE DIRECT," classified ads, numerology, and AIDS information. The classifieds on this occasion include a notice from one *travelo*, age twenty-five, looking for another to go to Tunisia for a month's vacation (the plane tickets are already reserved). A thirty-five-year-old man living on the outskirts of Paris seeks an *"amie"* who would take pleasure in dressing him in her clothes and her underwear. There are invitations to parties—for *"travelos sympathiques"* interested in an "exchange of ideas," for *"amateurs de lingerie."* There are fetishists—lovers of fur, of vinyl underpants, of paramilitary uniforms, of bridal gowns, of nineteen-sixties-style nylon blouses that button up the back—in search of others who might share their enthusiasms or play out their fantasies. "Sylvie" announces a *"boutique discrète,"* where drag queens can buy wigs, women's shoes, lingerie, and sexy outfits (some made to measure), by appointment. *Travelos* in Rennes, Montpelier, Toulouse, Brest, Epinal would like to find others in their neighborhoods. "Marie-Amélie" wants to know if there isn't someone out there who knows of a little hotel, maybe in the countryside or at the seashore, where one could spend a quiet weekend as a girl? The people behind the ads describe themselves: their age; their height; their build; their station in life (several *BCBG*s, or yuppies, and one *PDG*, or CEO); their personality (*"sympa et assez cool"*); their appearance, in some cases right down to the particulars (*"totalement épilée"*—completely shaved).

Option number two, BOÎTES AUX LETTRES, provides callers with electronic mailboxes for their replies.

Under the category labeled GRAFFITI are various messages, among them:

Métro Line 1

I saw you this morning on the Métro, you got on at Reuilly Diderot, there wasn't much doubt about your true nature. I couldn't approach you on account of my wife, who was on my arm. Our gazes often crossed and sometimes we even brushed up against each other, thanks to the movement of the train.

I can forget neither your perfume nor the look in your eyes.

I would like to meet you, to know you, maybe you come here on occasion, maybe we'll meet again in the Métro.

Or perhaps someone will recognize you and will want to leave me a message. Signed, Vasco.

Option number six, called TESTS, is in the tradition of the quizzes that have long been a popular staple of women's magazines trafficking in self-improvement. The multiple-choice questions manage to be at the same time soul-searching and vapid—a revelation only for those souls that have never been searched before.

> Your trump card in the game of seduction?
> A a casual attitude
> B savoir-faire
> C beauty
> D your immense culture

At times, the queries seem like mere filibuster, designed to keep the caller on the line at a charge of 1.29 francs per minute.

> An orange sheath with green spike heels . . .
> A . . . shocks you.
> B I adore it.
> C It's not very subtle.
> D I don't like those colors.

When every so often the tests tackle larger issues, they routinely
seem at a loss for larger answers.

> Virile or feminine, what's the difference?
> A different clothes
> B a state of mind
> C it's a question of temperament
> D it's hard to say

The responses provided are interesting in some cases for their wild
variety, in others, for their lack of it.

> What does a virile guy do?
> A he rushes in
> B he fights
> C he gives orders
> D he listens

> And a feminine woman, what does she do?
> A she smiles
> B she says yes
> C she submits
> D she acts like one of the guys

As an exercise in self-knowledge, the test purports to be geared
specifically to *travelos*.

> You feel most fully a woman . . .
> A in a miniskirt
> B in an evening gown
> C in a bodysuit
> D in all circumstances

> And when do you feel most fully a man?
> A never
> B at work
> C in street clothes
> D in an impeccable tuxedo

Even so, the fact remains that many of the questions, however psychologically rudimentary, are of the sort that people who have no urge to dress in the clothes of the opposite sex might never get around to asking themselves.

She looks more than ever like a man now that she is a woman. Indeed, it is impossible to believe that a person who shaves and has a beard; whose proportions and muscular development are herculean; who jumps in and out of a carriage without assistance and goes up stairs four steps at a time, belongs to the female sex.

> Contemporary newspaper account of
> the Chevalier d'Eon's appearances at
> the court of Versailles, quoted in *D'Eon
> de Beaumont: His Life and Time*

"Heavens!" she thought, "what fools they make of us—what fools we are!" And here it would seem from some ambiguity in her terms that she was censuring both the sexes equally, as if she belonged to neither; and indeed, for the time being she seemed to vacillate; she was man; she was woman; she knew the secrets, shared the weaknesses of each.

> VIRGINIA WOOLF,
> *Orlando*

Sara and Toni live together in Paris in a small apartment on a winding street not far from the Place Pigalle. "Sara" and "Toni" are not in fact their real names but the names of the characters they have invented for themselves. The people who play at being Sara and Toni are a couple in their mid-thirties: she's Spanish, he's French. They go to parties as Sara and Toni, to clubs, to events. When they travel, they pack Sara's and Toni's clothes as well as their own, so that they can take Sara and Toni along.

She dresses as a man dressed as a woman—a hapless drag queen trying to make it in show business, with "Sara" for a stage name. Whenever Sara performs, as she does sometimes in a bar in Madrid, disaster strikes: her heel breaks, her costume falls apart, the sound system goes on the fritz. But Sara is as undeterred by these calamities as she is by her own clumsiness and her apparent lack of talent. In the end, the audience and the people she meets feel sorry for her and want to help her; infuriating as she may be, she is even more pathetic. It is her determination that is so winning, that has seen her through a long, if flat, career—part of an elaborate past invented for her. According to this fictitious background, Sara has flopped everywhere, from a night-club in Las Vegas to small towns in the Spanish provinces. She sings Edith Piaf songs with a Spanish accent (the woman-who-dresses-as-a-man-who-dresses-as-Sara was born in Granada, raised in Madrid). Sara's wardrobe is flamboyant and extensive; a friend who runs a thrift shop on Second Avenue, in New York, is always on the lookout for clothes that suit her style.

The man who is the companion of the woman-dressed-as-a-man-who-dresses-as-Sara dresses as Toni—a man who does drag and does it far better than Sara. Even in drag, Toni goes by a male name, though it is not the name his parents gave him (which is French, as is he); he sees no contradiction in looking like a woman and being addressed as a man. Toni's character is not so complicated, with a past that hasn't been filled in. Mostly, he turns out for parties or goes to clubs or takes part in Halloween celebrations. Toni wears Sara's hand-me-downs.

The woman-dressed-as-a-man-who-dresses-as-Sara says that this wasn't some elaborate scheme on her part, that it just happened: one day, she put on the trappings of femininity—a blond wig, a siren dress, high heels—and she discovered that she looked not so much like a sexier woman but like a man in a woman's clothes. She attributes this to the fact that she's muscular, broad across the back and shoulders, with prominent biceps and deltoids, and that her features—a bold nose, a square jaw, black eyebrows—are made to seem completely incongruous when framed by a long blond wig. Even as a fourteen-year-old, she says, she looked the part: with an athletic build and no breasts, she was chosen from among her fellow class-mates—all girls—to play the role of a man in her convent school's theatrical production. Her mother came to see the show and didn't recognize her. Thanks to her dance training (she is a performer, with a flamenco company of her own), she has the capacity to alter her posture and her movement; as Sara, she forgoes the refined grace and lyricism that characterize her demeanor as a ballerina and allows herself to play out other possibilities—the blunt gestures, the weighted stance, a certain solidity—considered much more typical of men. Not only is Sara a man, she's a clumsy man, inept and perpetually flustered.

Toni says his character came about for some of the same reasons. Even when he's not dressed in drag, he claims, the people he meets often wonder whether he's a man or a woman. Sometimes, he explains, he chooses to suppress his feminine side, and then people take him for a man; at other times, he suppresses his masculine side, and then people take him for a woman. There is what he calls a "border"—a thin line separating the masculine and the feminine on the map of his personality, a line that is crossed, back and forth, repeatedly in the course of an ordinary day. And each time that happens, Toni claims, everything changes—not just his appearance and the way he walks but also the way he thinks. Toni believes that everyone has a masculine and a feminine side, and he considers himself unusual only to the extent that he has cultivated both rather than one at the expense of the other. He has taught himself how to manipulate the variables in order to control the impression he is making, precisely calibrating the degrees of masculinity and femininity. It was in Morocco, he says, where sexual ambiguity is "dangerous," that he first realized that by tying back his long hair, he would be taken for a man, whereas if he let it fall loose about his shoulders, he would be taken for a woman. But that, he says, is just one pathetically obvious example of the sort of small indicators people use to settle the rather large question of whether the individual at hand is a man or a woman.

In the early eighties, Sara and Toni lived in New York, where they met. Sara went to a party with a friend, and there was Toni, sitting in a corner. "Is that a woman or is that a man?" she asked her friend. Toni was looking at her seductively. He was dressed, she recalls, as a woman.

"I wasn't dressed *specifically* as a woman," he protests.

"Well," Sara replies, "you were dressed more as a woman than as a man."

Toni persists. "I didn't think of dressing up as a woman when I went to that party."

"I know," Sara says in a conciliatory tone.

"I just dressed the way I felt like dressing to go out to a party, without thinking as a man or as a woman."

"That's right," Sara says resignedly. "His hair was down, and he was wearing really tight pants and dangle earrings." She shrugs and laughs. "Like any man."

They talked for an hour, at the end of which, she says, she didn't care what he was. "She had to take me home to find out," Toni says.

To Sara's mind, the traditional sex roles are unrealistic, and they're ubiquitous, reinforced by television, magazines, and advertising. In the struggle to become the perfect woman or the perfect man, she says, so many people get lost along the way. For a long time, she raged against the stereotypes, until one day she decided to play with them instead.

According to Toni, it's easier to do drag if you take it to the extremes, as he does when he dresses up; then no one even suspects that he's a man. That way, what he calls "the discovery process"—the realization that this may not be a woman after all—unfolds gradually. It's when you begin to mix the stereotypes that you get into trouble, he says, and then people feel provoked or alarmed or threatened, right off. As bizarre as it seems, a man in drag who looks completely like a woman is reassuring by virtue of the fact that he upholds the rules by which we play, whereas someone who positions himself somewhere between the stereotypes, exploiting certain aspects of them and rejecting others, calls the established order into question. Sara believes that in most if not all Western societies, being a man is a privilege, and being a woman is not. By behaving as a woman, a man renounces the privilege, thereby, she says, insulting those who have held on to it.

The woman-dressed-as-a-man-who-dresses-as-Sara explains that Sara is a cartoon-style drag queen because that's what most drag queens are: when men dress as women, they dress as caricatures of women. This is a practice that the woman-dressed-as-a-man-who-dresses-as-Sara abhors. It's always women's worst qualities that get imitated, she complains—their vanity, their helplessness, their affectations, their stupidity. Nine times out of ten, drag transforms men into bimbos. Their true attitudes about women, which these days may be closely monitored in the presence of women, are laid bare, with no compunctions and no self-consciousness. The woman-dressed-as-a-man-who-dresses-as-Sara says she knows a drag queen in Madrid, a former priest with long hair, long nails, elaborate makeup, whose lovers treat her just like a woman to such an extent that they expect her to do the cleaning, the washing, and the shopping.

Toni is different from other drag queens, the woman-dressed-as-a-man-who-dresses-as-Sara claims, and she especially likes the fact that when he dresses up, he becomes someone who's cozy and supportive and compassionate, she says, as real woman are.

Barbette is popular with those who see in him a woman, with those who intuit that he is a man, and with others, whose souls are moved by the supernatural sex of beauty.

JEAN COCTEAU,
Le Numéro Barbette

The tourists who constitute the audience for the shows in the drag bars on the rue Fontaine arrive in buses that move at a crawl through the narrow streets of the Second Arrondissement. Jovial-looking men and women from small towns all over France, dressed in the clothes they ordinarily save for Sundays or in outfits bought especially for this vacation, move through the streets en masse, clogging the sidewalks. They are the aunts and uncles of young people who have migrated to Paris to pursue a career that would have been impossible back home—something to do with government, or fashion, or music, or art. Seated in rows at long tables perpendicular to the stage, the visitors to Paris sip champagne and watch the floor show, which is remarkably chaste considering that its subject matter is sex. They laugh at the jokes, nodding in agreement, congratulating themselves and one another on their sophistication. This is a trip they've been looking forward to for months, ever since they booked it and convinced their friends to come along; they travel in couples. And now here they are, having a good time, just as they knew they would. This is the essence of being in Paris, the capital of the world, where everything happens. This is what it means to be out on the town.

From one bar to the next—Mme. Arthur's (the most famous), Le Dépanneur, Le Carrousel, Michou, the Divan Japonais (named for an Yvette Guilbert song)—the shows are similar and predictable. The ceiling is always low; the decor is red velvet, a dim reference to the li-

PLATE 25

PLATE 26

PLATE 27

PLATE 28

PLATE 29

PLATE 30

PLATE 31

PLATE 32

PLATE 33

PLATE 34

PLATE 35

PLATE 36

PLATE 37

PLATE 38

PLATE 39

centiousness and the luxury of the Belle Epoque. The front door is locked, and the customer rings a bell for admittance, as if this were a speakeasy and the contraband was not even sex itself but jokes about it. Prohibition was an American phenomenon, however, and the notion of banning any of life's sustaining pleasures would find few, if any, adherents here.

The entertainment consistently evokes the heyday of the French chanteuse, a species that no longer exists in its own right but lives on in drag re-creations and lip-synching. The star of the show, a vivacious blonde, talks in a deep voice, with no apologies for disrupting the illusion she has so meticulously created by virtue of her grandiose evening gown, her rhinestone jewelry, her long wig. She singles out a man seated at the edge of the stage and compliments him on his tie. She delivers a monologue about the loneliness of the career girl, who is depicted as misguided and miserable. Keeping an eye on her reflection in the mirrors along one wall, she mouths the words to a Shirley Bassey recording, while in the upstage corner a man with a trumpet pretends to play the accompaniment on the soundtrack. For the final chorus, she incites the audience to clap along. Eventually, in a performance oddly lacking in titillation, she strips down to her sequined G-string and performs a can-can and a series of inane high kicks. The emcee, a brunette with silicone breasts, turns to the audience and demands, triumphantly: "What is the difference between a man and a woman?" The audience cheers. Her sermon continues, extolling "the glory of Woman" and naming a beautiful woman "the symbol of our joie de vivre." These are the drag queens that Lola and her friends refer to as "serious," as "professional"—those who go about the business of their daily lives as women and work as entertainers in the bars to support themselves. Their fashion sense is scant. Their style, to Lola's way of thinking, is more provincial than Parisian, without the chic that so many French women cultivate over the course of a lifetime. These are not the drag queens one sees at the Folies Pigalle on a Saturday night, or at Les Bains on Tuesdays, or at Le Boy on Thursdays, or at Queen, a club on the Champs-Elysées, where drag queens from London congregate. These drag queens keep to themselves, and, Lola says with pride, she and her friends have absolutely nothing in common with them.

The drag acts that occupy the spotlight at the tourist bars in Montmartre are, for most if not all of the members of the audience, nothing less than what they expected. They think of drag as burlesque—the broadest, most obvious humor, amusing to a point but limited in its possibilities. The specter of Barbette (born Vander Clyde, in Round Rock, Texas), who in the 1930s mesmerized Paris audiences with his drag trapeze act, has been banished to New York, where in 1994 a performance artist by the name of John Kelly resuscitated Barbette's reputation in a work that paid tribute to him.

Although other trapeze artists, acrobats, and at least one juggler working in circuses in France in the nineteenth century dressed in drag, as women, as a way of making their stunts appear more spectacular, Barbette's act was remarkable not so much for its virtuosity as for what contemporary witnesses called its feminine polish and elegance. At the end, according to Jean Cocteau's admiring account, after the fifth curtain call, Barbette removed his wig, exposing in a single gesture "the unforgettable lie" of his performance. "After having reaped the applause for his success as a gymnast," Cocteau wrote, "he must reap the applause for his success as an actor." The audience was dumbfounded to see the illusion of a woman turn so abruptly into a man. And then came the tour de force: Barbette rolled his shoulders, extended his hands, flexed his muscles, exaggerated the sportive swagger of a golfer—demonstrating that masculinity, like femininity, is a role, a performance.

The intelligence and subtlety that Barbette brought to the business of impersonating a woman has largely been lost. If that level of drag— ironic and thought-provoking—still exists in Paris, it exists in the clubs, in drag as it is practiced by Lola and her friends. It has moved into the realm of nightlife, having seceded from the theater. None of the so-called stars of the current shows stands a chance of attaining the status of a hero, of staking out a place in the culture, as Barbette did. Here, on the tiny platform stages of the cabarets listed in the guidebooks, drag has become sheer mindless entertainment.

Not far from this beaten path, at a bar called Maine, the clientele is overwhelmingly female. A stained-glass panel, backlit, depicts two women together. The pinlights in the ceiling are dimly trained on a small dance floor populated by pairs of women wearing men's suits and tuxedos. Around the perimeter runs a velvet banquette from which other women look on impassively, sipping their drinks. Their conversation is concertedly low, pitched in a register different from the chirping soprano so many French women affect.

A party of four—three women dressed as men, escorted by a man sporting a mustache—is shown to a table in the corner. Eventually, the women get up and move to the middle of the floor; the man stays behind, lights a cigarette, smokes it slowly. At arm's length, ballroom-dance style, his friends shift their weight from foot to foot in a tentative two-step, seeming as ill at ease as teenage boys. On a Saturday night when the bars that feature men dressed as women are doing a sellout business, this one feels strangely deserted. Were it not for the feeble turnout (no more than twenty, all told) and the incongruous music (the Village People singing "YMCA"), the setting might recall the private drag clubs where Colette and her friends congregated to declare their freedom from the feminine conventions of their time. But here the defiance seems diminished, not so much collective as individual, and the sense of women arrogating the rights of men by dressing like them is missing entirely. The iconoclasm pioneered by Colette and her circle gave way eventually to a more superficial but no less compelling glamour that persisted around women in drag well into the forties, when the central characters of Alberto Moravia's novel *The Conformist* finish off an evening in Paris with a visit to a lesbian nightclub where the women are dressed as men. The fascination of that scene is gone now. A spectator studies these women, with their cropped hair, their dapper suits, their ties, and thinks not of Colette's eyewitness descriptions but of Helmut Newton's hard-edged sirens in smoking jackets designed by Yves Saint Laurent, or of patrician-looking women dressed like bankers in three-piece, pin-striped suits in Ralph Lauren's ad campaigns. The image of a woman—independent, dressed as a man, breaking the rules—has been co-opted by fashion, and what once seemed startling now comes across as merely stylish in some instances and even démodé in others. A fifteen-minute floor show, with overtones of S&M, is presided over by an emcee wearing an abbreviated turquoise stretch dress and fishnet stockings. The sole representative of the feminine ideal in this context, she turns out to be a drag queen.

Across the Seine in Montparnasse, L'Ange Bleu has the aspect of a train station at rush hour. The crowd at the bar is four-deep; couples dance to canned disco music in the space between the little tables. In the far corner, the scowling proprietors keep an eye out for trouble. The drag queens—mostly black and Asian, wearing long wigs and minidresses and carrying clutch bags—scan the room, wasting no time on conversation. Burly men in rumpled work clothes or trig French army uniforms buy them drinks, dance with them, leave with them. The turnover is quick; few customers stay the evening.

Despite—or perhaps because of—all the usual interdictions, prostitution in Paris has been dignified by a level of intellectual debate that is reserved in other cultures for more "respectable" topics. Baudelaire, for one, was fascinated by prostitution in his time, as Foucault and Barthes have been in ours. Manet and Degas apotheosized whores in their paintings; Brassai, in his photographs. Marcel Duchamp invented for himself an alter ego by the name of Rrose Selavy (*Eros, c'est la vie*); dressed as a bourgeois lady, wearing pearls and a hat, he posed for an "advertisement" for a perfume of his own invention, called Belle Haleine—fresh breath. Anglo-Saxon countries, with their puritanical misgivings about the body and its gratification, may concern themselves with prostitution in all its political ramifications: issues of power and money and oppression. But in France, it seems, the discourse gravitates more toward the esthetic dimension. *"Esthétiques de la Prostitution,"* a daylong symposium held at the Ecole des Beaux Arts in 1993, brought together a number of highly respected scholars and writers to deliver lectures, among them: *"La prostituée surréaliste"* and *"L'esthétique du comportement."* The program, with a subtitle that translates as "On Art as Prostitution and on Prostitution as Art," was organized by Alberto Sorbelli—a young Italian artist living in Paris, a former student of Peter Halley, the American painter. Sorbelli's own work lately revolves around the theme of prostitution, always in drag.

He says that he dresses for his work *en femme* because a man in drag is instantly presumed to be a whore, whereas a man or a woman in the clothes of his or her own sex, no matter how provocative, may be given the benefit of the doubt. In Paris, he attends gallery openings, where the owners turn him away. "There's nothing that would interest you here," one woman assured him. He appears at the first-night party for the Salon de Mars, and the organizers summon the police to remove him from the premises. Sorbelli considers the intervention part of the performance. His aim, he says, is to call attention to the limits on people's "access to art"—who has it, who doesn't. This is not drag for its own sake but drag for the sake of art.

On the street, in the Métro, at cafés, Sorbelli scrutinizes women—their hair, their makeup, their laughs, their mannerisms, their postures. He inspects their appearance for clues to what qualifies them as women. Over time, he has come to the conclusion that though certain women can be quite feminine, a man dressed as a woman can be even more feminine—"exquisitely feminine," as Sorbelli sees it—because femininity is artifice. Sorbelli describes the projects that women have historically undertaken for the sake of their appearance as long and tiresome, "a lot of work, at the very least"—too much, given the lives women now lead. Busy women without the time to devote to clothes shopping and the hair salon have defaulted on the feminine position as we have known it, leaving a vacuum. Enter drag queens, to fill it. Photographs and movies have propagated this glamorous ideal, creating an alternate reality that takes the barest outline of a woman as a starting point and ends with the image of a goddess. If, as Sorbelli contends, this fantasy has as little to do with women—living, breathing female human beings—as it does with men, then it is fair game for anyone, of either sex, to assume.

A young man in his late twenties—I'll call him Hervé—who has worked the Bois de Boulogne as a prostitute, in drag, draws a distinction between the way the *travelos* dress in the bars, the cabarets, the nightclubs, and the way they dress in the Bois. Unlike the stars of the cabaret shows or the drag queens who turn out for the club scene, he has no need of a female pseudonym. The people he meets when he's dressed as a woman are not interested in making conversation. Hervé says that the drag queens in the bars and the clubs aim to look dazzling, with a kind of drop-dead chic (they refer to one another, playfully, as *"créatures"*), while his colleagues in the Bois have a harder-edged style. They wear black leather, thick makeup, torn fishnet stockings—"sexy, with S&M overtones" is his description—not unlike the way the real women who work as prostitutes dress. Likewise, this is the way Sorbelli dresses for his "performances," in the image of the drag queens who are whores—despite his studious attentions to the way women present themselves, despite his theories about femininity not belonging exclusively to women but having passed into the public domain.

Among the drag queens in the Bois, Hervé is something of a pariah. He breaks rank, his colleagues feel, by wearing clothes that are more glamorous than provocative, advertising style over sex—an approach that would seem to go against all common sense, as far as business is concerned. But Hervé's originality has paid off: not only has he managed to set himself apart from the competition but, dressed in a pink plastic dress with big earrings and a teased hairdo right out of the sixties, he proved to be more visible by dark than his neighbors dressed in black.

A nighttime joy ride through the Bois has become a popular after-dinner pastime for curious bourgeois Parisians, most of whom are just looking. Parked at intervals are trucks selling French fries. From time to time, the police stage raids, which are always highly publicized. In 1992, in an ostentatious campaign to rid the Bois of prostitution by means of deterring customers who arrived by car, the police barricaded certain roads through the park, but not before informing some fifty members of the international press, who covered the event. This grandstanding, billed at the time as a measure to curtail the spread of AIDS, didn't last long, however, and within a few months the park's after-dark population was back to what it had been before the police intervened. Hervé says that the drag queens have pretty much taken over the Bois and chased the women out. After the police sweep, two of the few remaining women who worked the Bois complained in an interview with a reporter for one of the daily papers that it was the prostitutes in drag, with their drugs and their thievery, who had ruined the Bois for the rest of them, scaring off their good customers of long standing, who were honest citizens. Eventually, having ceded the Bois to the drag queens (just as they had previously ceded the Place Pigalle), the women moved on to the Bois de Vincennes, to the Place des Ternes, to the boulevards in the more fashionable neighborhoods.

Hervé says that when he first went to work as a prostitute in Paris, he dressed as a young boy (he was twenty-six at the time but looked like a teenager). The money was good, but then, as anonymous sex became increasingly available in gay bars and clubs, the rates went down. So Hervé began to dress as a woman. In drag, he explains, prostitutes charge less than they could if they were working as boys, but they have more clients in the course of a night, which works out to more money in the end. Hervé says that his clients are heterosexual—husbands and fathers on the way home to their families in the suburbs. He claims that he finds it easier to work as a woman, because it allows him to believe that the person he becomes every night, out there in a skirt, stopping traffic, isn't really him. *En femme*, he has become more audacious, doing things that he insists he would never do as himself, as a man.

By his own account, Hervé first dressed in drag at the age of twelve, for a talent show at his school in his hometown in Provence. He dressed as Jane Birkin and sang a Jane Birkin song. The audience of parents, teachers, and fellow students was appalled. Even after all these years, he is mystified by their response. A boy becomes Jane Birkin or, as in the case of one of Hervé's classmates, Julius Caesar—the one seems to him no more absurd than the other.

Hervé now gets most of his clothes from a friend, a stylish woman who wears the same size and passes on her castoffs. He claims that he has no desire to spend the money he earns on his drag wardrobe, unlike the *travelos* who hold court late at night in the clubs in Pigalle. He has been there, dressed as a man, with his friends. He has seen them. He recalls some of those who were the most popular, who made the biggest impressions—reigning divas like Zaza TGV, named for France's high-speed train, and La Grande Esmeralda, whose pseudonym qualifies as a backhanded homage to Victor Hugo. Hervé admires these drag queens who look so convincing as women, but he reserves his greatest admiration for those who can transform themselves instantly from a convincing woman to a convincing man. When he works, he wears several pairs of stockings, in layers; he refuses to shave or wax his legs, or pluck his eyebrows, as many drag queens do, because, he says, then one looks bizarre when one *isn't* in drag. Hervé is intent on retaining his identity as a man.

A wistfulness pervades his voice when he talks about dressing as a woman. He acknowledges the element of nostalgia inherent in it—a longing for a simpler time, when the distinctions between the sexes were stark. Whether this has something to do with men and their mothers, he says, he isn't sure, although he has thought about it and remarks on the fact that, in a Courrèges minidress, with his hair teased into a bubble, he is dressed in the style his mother wore at the height of the sixties, during his childhood. More than most drag queens, Hervé has a keen appreciation of the irony that underlies their efforts: that a group of men who have broken with the society in which they were raised because they found its criteria for masculinity impossibly narrow, if not downright ludicrous, have devoted themselves to the ritual observance of that masculinity's opposite number—a femininity that is no less oppressive.

....

In roughly half of the pictures in his modeling portfolio, J. Alexander, a.k.a. Jay, appears as a man, dressed in funky suits by pioneer designers like Yohji Yamamoto and Jean Paul Gaultier; in the rest of the pictures Jay is seen in drag, as a woman, wearing impossibly chic cocktail dresses and evening gowns by Emanuel Ungaro, Yves Saint Laurent, and other couturiers who occupy the pinnacle of high fashion. Slender, six feet three, with black skin, and hair that has been straightened and shingled, Jay looks equally persuasive as a man and as a woman. More incongruous than his capacity to play the part of both sexes, however, is the kind of woman he chooses to play. Leafing through the pages of his portfolio, even the most casual observer can't help noticing what a mismatch this man and this woman—who are the same person—appear to be: the man, a young renegade, alert to the latest shifts in the zeitgeist; the woman, a self-satisfied figurehead of the ruling class, clothed in the accoutrements of luxury and leisure. If ever by some coincidence these two people were to meet, they would surely have nothing to say to each other.

Born Alexander Jenkins, in the South Bronx, J. Alexander now lives in Paris and, in between his own modeling jobs, serves as a consultant to other models, teaching them to stride the catwalk with authority and grace. His students, for the most part, have been girls who started out in front of the camera and, having made a name for themselves on the covers of magazines, suddenly find themselves in demand on the runway. Their agencies call Jay. Among the success stories he claims as his alumnae are Claudia Mason, Susan Holmes, Meghan Douglas, Nadia Auerman, Tyra Banks, Tatiana Patitz, Jennifer Flavin, Patricia Hartman, and Valerie Jean. Naomi Campbell and Karen Mulder ask him how they did after a show; he gives them corrections, the way an acting coach dispenses suggestions after the curtain goes down. The fact that Jay has less professional experience than most of the girls he trains seems to bother neither him nor them. Nor, evidently, does the somewhat holier-than-thou aspect—the insinuation that a man might be better at being a woman than a woman. And now, here he is, offering his expertise for the benefit of those who need a little remedial work. He has come by the knowledge he imparts not so much by experience as by imagination—by identifying with models, by imitating them (he has an extensive repertory of impersonations). "Femininity is an act," he says.

The lessons take place in a studio he rents in the Twentieth Arrondissement, and they are strictly private—no mothers, no agents, no boyfriends. Instead of a runway, the models walk the length of a red-carpet runner, "to make them feel a little more regal," Jay says. The first hour is in flats, with no music, to get the girls comfortable and into some natural rhythm; then he asks them to move to music; then he asks them to change into high heels.

"With most girls, the problem is posture," Jay explains. "They need to be told what to do at the end of the runway, how to pose, where to place their hands, where to look. 'Just keep your head up and look straight ahead,' I tell them. 'Looking at the fashion editors is not gonna get you on the cover of their magazines.' " He scrutinizes the way the girls walk and zeroes in on their awkward idiosyncrasies. Girls who are heavy on their heels are taught to walk leading with the toes. "And then you get girls who know they have to lose weight, so they don't move their hips because they're afraid it'll call attention to them." Jay says that he tries to help his students make the clothes they wear come alive. "Maybe I get this from my drag training," he laughs. "But I think to myself: If I wore that dress, I would move it like this. Or: I'd unbutton that coat from the bottom up."

Jay gives the girls instruction in how to vary their walks for different designers. "For Rei Kawakubo and Yohji Yamamoto, you basically walk straight out—no expression, no hip movement, no turns. The clothing is the star. At Ungaro, you drop certain coats or capes and let them hang from the elbow; you remove one glove and hold it in your hand; you take off a jacket and fist it on your hip. Saint Laurent likes you to drag the coats. Givenchy and Valentino want you to make the clothes move. Montana expects you to be serious and a little more dramatic, with more posing. Gaultier is looser, more fun. And at Chanel, where the girls come out really fast, one right after the other, I tell them to just use their personalities and make it work."

He shows them how to take off a coat without fumbling and then carry it, draped over one arm. He counsels them in tactics for dealing with runway emergencies: how to handle the situation if you're doing "doubles" (two girls at a time), you pivot and pose, and then discover that your partner has kept right on walking and left you behind ("Let her go, you do your own thing"). He teaches them professionalism ("If I'm assigned a dress I don't like, you'll never know it"). When he demonstrates the difference between how to move in a taffeta dress and how to move in a chiffon dress, he becomes a woman in his gestures, and the girls who are his students do their best to imitate him.

Jay's aptitude for fashion first manifested itself when, as a child, he sewed dresses out of his father's socks. After high school, he went to work as a stock boy at Bergdorf Goodman, in the designer sportswear department; when the floor got busy, he says, he would "charm the women and sell the clothes," until finally he was promoted to the rank of salesperson. His first runway appearance, however unofficial, was in 1983, when Claude Montana staged a show at the armory. Jay bought a ticket and went dressed in a ball gown. When, a few minutes before the proceedings got under way, the velvet ropes that cordoned off the runway were removed, he saw his chance, leapt onto the catwalk, and stalked it twice—posing at the beginning, the middle, and the end—and then exited to wild applause. When *Women's Wear Daily* and *The Village Voice* ran articles about the event, Jay was mentioned. And then, in 1985, Jean Paul Gaultier staged a show in New York, using men and women found on the street as models, and Jay was hired—as a man.

He contends that the difference between walking down a runway and walking down the street is that the runway calls for a little more attitude. "You get to move your body more," he explains. His own training ground was the New York club scene, "where it was okay to be anything," he says. "The discotheques were our runway." Years of going to Xenon or Area or the Palladium or the Boy Bar, dressed in something outlandish, have paid off, in the confidence models need to put themselves on display. Even so, Jay claims that most drag in New York these days—the big wigs, the platform shoes—is too theatrical for his taste. "The people who are doing it, it's great for them, and I can admire it," he says. "But, for me—I just like pretty things."

Jay's favorite designer is Gianfranco Ferré, particularly Ferré's collections for the house of Dior, in which he evoked the haughty glamour of the fifties. "I think it was their good couture dresses that made women of that era sit the way they did, so straight and tall," Jay hypothesizes, demonstrating fifties posture as he talks. "You couldn't collapse, because the boning and corsets and things were built into the dress—it was holding you up. And you have to sit like this"—here, he crosses his legs and shifts his weight to the side of one thigh—"because you have a big bustle. Or, you have to sit like this"—and he scoots forward to the edge of his chair—"because there's a bouquet of silk flowers at the back of your dress, and you don't want to squish them." Jay dreams of modeling in a fashion show for one of the Paris haute couture houses. That, to his mind, would be the ultimate achievement. He seems persuaded that it's bound to happen, sooner or later. "Something inside of me says that it's just around the corner," he insists.

In the meantime, he continues to go to castings for fashion shows and shoots, though never in drag. "I mean, that to me would defeat the whole purpose. This is how I look, this is me—I am your canvas." Jay dresses in drag only for an actual booking and, on rare occasions, for some fancy social event. Every year for nine years running he attended the black-tie benefit for the Metropolitan Museum's Costume Institute, dressed in an evening gown; he has also turned up in drag at what he calls "snobbish sit-down dinners," an accomplishment of which he is especially proud. "I think it's more of a challenge to sit at a table and actually talk to people than to go to any old restaurant and make a scene by overdoing it and being loud and outrageous. I mean, I'm loud enough as it is: six feet three plus with high heels on, and my French twist, and all this fabric hanging behind me—I think it speaks for itself. I attract attention just by walking into a room." He claims that he has no desire whatsoever to be a woman. "I want to be able to change back and forth, from one extreme to the other, and just be comfortable," he explains. "Have to be a woman now?" He snaps his fingers. "No problem!" He says that once he starts putting on makeup, everything changes—the way he holds his mouth, the way he moves.

Jay believes that the difference between being credible as a woman and being a caricature of a woman is for the most part a psychological one, and when he is dressed in drag, he tries to be one hundred percent feminine in his head. To the extent that being a woman is an act, being a man is one, too, he concedes. "I'm constantly reminding myself not to move my hips," he says. "No hips! And keep your feet firmly planted on the ground." Male models, too, ask his advice about how to move, how to carry a coat, how to work with a girl. He gives them the same cardinal rule that he gives his female clients: "You have two chances," he tells them—"one to make an impression, and one to clean it up."

Check your ego at the door, Jay instructs his clients, cover girls included. Inside the studio, working one on one, he is unfazed by celebrity. "Everyone's the same," he maintains. "Your tits are bigger, yours are bought, yours are natural. You had more surgery. You're dyeing your hair. You make less money." Jay claims that on a few occasions, a model has offered him a bribe to refuse to coach another girl—either as an attempt to stave off competition or as a result of some personal vendetta. Then, Jay says, he behaves in the best Jessica Hahn tradition: he takes the money, and he teaches the other girl anyway.

[Louis XIV's brother, called "Monsieur,"] opened [the ball] with Mademoiselle de Brancas who was very pretty (she later became the Princesse d'Harcourt), and a moment later he went to dress up as a woman and returned to the ball masked. Everyone recognized him, just as he intended, and the Chevalier de Lorraine tendered him his hand. He danced the minuet and then went to sit amongst all the ladies. . . . It is impossible to describe the extent of his coquetry in admiring himself. . . . But perhaps I would have been worse. Men, once they think they are beautiful, are far more besotted with their appearance than women are.

The Transvestite Memoirs of the Abbé de Choisy

The French, with their acute sense of history, are not easily shocked or impressed. Gustave Flaubert and George Sand are known to have dressed in drag; why not the guy who lives upstairs? Lola's command of the Folies Pigalle on a Saturday night is put into a certain perspective when considered alongside accounts of Louis XIV's brother in drag, leading off a ball at Versailles. The notion of J. Alexander coaching fashion models in their walks is no more preposterous than the fact that the Abbé de Choisy, a seventeenth-century clergyman who dressed as a woman, instructed a live-in pupil in the practice of femininity, providing lessons in fashion, flower arrangement, and table settings. Nor do Sara and Toni seem all that peculiar a couple in light of Choisy's marriage—to a woman who dressed as a man. The arrest, in 1983, in Paris, of a Chinese opera star and his lover, a French spy who for eighteen years believed the Chinese man to be not only a woman but the mother of his child, inspired widespread fascination and *M. Butterfly*, a Broadway play. As, in its own time, did the sensational case of the Chevalier d'Eon de Beaumont, a member of Louis XV's secret service: resplendent in gowns by Rose Bertin, the queen's dressmaker, he not only dressed as a woman but claimed to be one, inciting such controversy that in London, where he had served as the king's diplomatic envoy, enormous wagers were made as to his true sex—a matter laid to rest only, finally, by his autopsy.

It is all the more remarkable, then, that Michel Cressol and his cohorts in the early seventies took Parisians by surprise, if not quite by storm. A writer for *Libération*, one of Paris's left-leaning daily newspapers, Cressol looks back on the founding of the movement—if that's not too precise a word for it—that came to be known by its delirious battle cry: *"Gazoline!"* In the aftermath of the student protests of 1968, the young political left had been commandeered by a band of macho advocates for revolution; Cressol was one of a group consisting of women (including, in some cases, the macho leaders' wives) and gay men who, having been shut out of the revolution (*"une contradiction totale,"* he says), founded FHAR, the Front Homosexuel de l'Action Révolutionnaire. In what he characterizes as an almost visceral reaction to the dictatorial style of the leaders who inspired their revolt, the founding members of FHAR espoused anarchy. Cressol describes it as a politics of refusal—the refusal of all organization, of bureaucracy, of leadership.

Within this conclave dedicated to refusal, the most vociferous were those who formed Gazoline. At FHAR's weekly meetings, at the Ecole des Beaux Arts—meetings that rapidly degenerated into endless debates—the Gazolines would interrupt, shouting insults, distributing madeleines (there was also hashish at the door), taking FHAR's policies to the extreme: the refusal of all discourse, of any representation, and, finally, of any action. It was a way of life, Cressol says, a way of doing nothing. At the start, they numbered around thirty. Some of them had occasional jobs; most of them, like Cressol, had parents in the provinces who sent them money from time to time (Paris was cheap in those days, he explains, and it was easy to live on very little). Dressed in drag—in weird outfits they'd found at the flea markets, or in bikinis—the Gazolines would systematically disrupt the solemnity of the strikes staged by the labor unions, running through the workers' midst and shouting the name of their movement or imbecilic questions, like "Where's the beach?"

In those days, Cressol continues, the drag scene in Paris pretty much revolved around Cochinelle, one of the pioneers of a generation of transsexuals who took hormones and saved up for surgery in Casablanca. Drag queens were required by law to work and to show the stubs of their paychecks when they were stopped by the police, as proof that they weren't prostitutes. Cochinelle made a name for herself as an entertainer; her wedding—in a church—was widely covered by the press. But the Gazolines' heroine was Marie-France, who in the seventies achieved the status of a pop star; she worked at the Alcazar, a cabaret for transsexuals. According to Cressol, she was so ravishing that people would stop in the street just to look at her. She also had a lot of style, a great fashion sense. She was one of the first to revive platform shoes in the seventies, he says, and in no time everyone else was wearing them too.

Eventually, the feeling within Gazoline was that it was no longer legitimate to play at being a drag queen, that the time had come to get serious—a sentiment that paralleled the influx of leftist students into the factories, to become blue-collar workers. Cressol says that some of his fellow members in the movement began taking hormones; he did not. Several of them became prostitutes, but, he explains, it was an intellectual and poetic kind of prostitution: they recited verse as they worked; they were regarded as bizarre, even (or perhaps especially) by their customers. Meanwhile, the Ecole des Beaux Arts had kicked out FHAR.

Ironically, Cressol says, in Paris as elsewhere, the drag queens of the seventies fell victim to the internal politics of the gay liberation movement. Gay men came out of the closet and locked the crazies in behind them, keeping the key in the pocket of their macho jeans. Cressol sees the "clone" look that prevailed among gay men in those days—the muscle T-shirt, the jeans, the construction boots—as another kind of drag, in and of itself. He claims that the prejudice against drag queens runs deeper than the clothes, that it reflects contempt for men who assume the passive role in sex, and that this bias is not French but universal. If drag queens in the nineties have become more public and aggressive, he figures it's because they've been denied the openness that gay liberation ushered in. And now it's their turn.

What has become of drag is in keeping with what has become of the rest of the culture, Cressol believes. Drag queens, like artists and architects and fashion designers, are caught up in the postmodern predicament: all styles, all references are accessible at any given moment. Thanks to the media, we are awash in images of every era that has preceded us, and as a result the style of our own time, if there is one, is a kind of pastiche that borrows elements from disparate periods and relies on their meaningful or witty juxtaposition. In drag, we see a fashion retrospective: aspects of the past, selectively revived and thoughtfully reassembled.

The idea, advanced by postmodernist scholars and critics, that gender, too, is pastiche—that femininity and masculinity are constellations of ritualized gestures we've acquired from our parents, ads, the movies—finds a premature champion in Claude Cahun, a French writer and photographer (born Lucy Schwob), who died in 1954. Often compared to Cindy Sherman, Cahun took pictures of herself as a man, as a woman, as various characters of indeterminate sex. Her photo-collages, in which we see a column of mouths or an agglomeration of eyes, lifted from the context of the faces to which they belong, dismantle the edifice of our uniqueness: our distinguishing features, seen in isolation, turn out to be interchangeable. Even the particulars of anatomy in Cahun's work are reduced to signs: impersonating a male bodybuilder, she wears a jersey pullover with two nipples appliquéd on the chest.

In an essay for the catalogue accompanying an exhibition of Cahun's work at the Musée de l'Art Moderne in Paris in 1995, François Leperlier cites "bovary-ism"—the principle articulated by the French critic Jules de Gaultier and named for Flaubert—by which, in the process of imagining oneself as being otherwise, one discovers one's true identity. "The quest for authenticity," Leperlier concludes, "plays a part in the act of self-creation, in a metamorphosis of the self." Some drag queens would argue that the truth lies not in the clay itself but in what the sculptor makes of it; and in their case, as in Cahun's, the sculptor also happens to *be* the clay; the self becomes the work of art. In the same exhibition catalogue, Elisabeth Lebovici writes of Cahun's capacity to take on so many different identities, not one of them more natural-seeming or "genuine" than the next. And this multiplicity, Lebovici notes, proves to be far more disturbing than mere transvestism—than the sight of Radclyffe Hall, say, or any number of other modern "amazons" dressed as men. In Cahun's work, and in the perpetual transformation of many latter-day drag queens, the self does not cohere; it does not begin as a whole and become increasingly fractured with each new identity it assumes. Instead, the self accrues: it is the sum total of all these identities, evenly weighed.

Cahun's name is often, inevitably, paired with Pierre Molinier's. Her approximate contemporary (though he outlived her by some twenty years), Molinier produced a vast body of work, including paintings, photographs, graphic art, and poems—much of it erotic, nearly all of it esoteric. His photographs—of himself, dressed in women's corsets and garter belts, sheer black seamed stockings, spike heels, masks, veils, blindfolds, wigs, and doll-like makeup—catalogue his fetishes. At his home in Bordeaux, he poses in a reproduction Louis XV armchair, or in front of a toile de Jouy–covered screen, or with other pieces of mass-reproduced bourgeois furniture, documenting the permutations of his lust in dramatic, high-contrast black-and-white. "From the beginning of my life," Molinier wrote, "I have had a transvestite soul." Even so, as the protagonist of his photographs, Molinier is seen sometimes as a woman (oddly shaped, it must be said, with a bouffant hairdo and a blank, expressionless face), sometimes as a creature who combines the erotic equipment and the obsessions of both sexes. The latter are more shocking at first glance; the former, more unsettling upon closer inspection. Molinier's portraits of himself as a woman also make use of a department-store mannequin, often disassembled, in pieces. But whether the blank, doll-like face belongs to the dummy or to Molinier is not clear. Whose torso are we looking at? Whose legs? The woman in the image is a composite of artificial parts—some belonging to a man, some to a mannequin—and they are eerily, equally valid.

Baudelaire's dictum, placing femininity and nature at odds with each other, relies on a certain complicity. If femininity is in fact artifice, and if—whether practiced by men in drag or by women—that artifice is ultimately convincing, then the viewer is also implicated. Accounts of the espionage case that eventually served as the basis for *M. Butterfly*, the long-running Broadway play, invariably raised the question: How could Bernard Boursicot, a clerk in the foreign service, have believed that the Chinese man to whom he had made love on countless occasions was a woman? Recounting the circumstances in *The New York Times Magazine*, Joyce Wadler wrote: "A naïve or credulous lover, looking at this man now, might believe he was looking at a woman. Of course, one could not look too closely. It was only illusion. But ninety percent of love, even a man of science will volunteer, is illusion. In defense of love, a story we love, a person we love, is there anyone among us who has not closed his eyes and refused to see?"

The refusal to see what stands before us is crucial if we are to focus instead on the image in our minds. The deception rests not so much on a willingness to suspend disbelief as on an active desire to do so. The drag queen and the onlooker become co-conspirators, engaged in the same, mutually agreed-upon fiction. Nowhere, perhaps, is the onlooker such an active participant as in France, where eroticism is venerated as a feat of the imagination.

AESTHETICS

Who do you want me to be?
Who do you want me to be?
I could be this,
I could be that.
I could be this,
I could be that.
I could be anything.
I could be him,
I could be her.
I could be him,
I could be her.
This.   That.   This.   That.
I could be a he,
I could be a she.
I could be a he,
I could be a she.
Who do you think I am?

ANDROGYNY,
"I Could Be This"

It's Kinky Gerlinky night in London, and some three thousand club-goers from all over England have converged on the Empire Ballroom in Leicester Square. The theme this Saturday in early June is "Carnival in Rio." The chartered buses pull up to the police barricades, and in single file their passengers disembark, looking slightly dazed and somewhat creased. An Indian chief in a gold lamé G-string fluffs the feathers on his headdress.

Gerlinda Costiff, who, along with her husband, Michael, organizes Kinky Gerlinky, has resurrected the outfit she wore for Carnaval on their trip to Brazil in February. Carnaval this evening is, of course, not so much an event as a concept, and it seems no less timely or fervent now in London than it did then in Rio, during that last hedonistic gasp in the days leading up to Ash Wednesday. The dance floor is populated with myriad Carmen Mirandas outfitted with platform sandals, tinsel, fans, feathers, balloons; the fruit motif is rampant. A guy with a boa of lemons and limes slung over his shoulders does the lambada. From the balcony, the view includes a turban decked with cherries and pearls; the cherries bob and sway in time to the music. A muscle-man in a Josephine Baker–style banana skirt stands at the bar—a spectator for the time being, as the finalists in the competition for best costume take the stage. Briefly, the spotlight is conferred on each contestant. Number 1—his body serving as a mere pedestal for the towering compote of oranges, grapefruits, cantaloupes, and soccer balls perched on top of his head—elicits wild applause. In the end, however, it's number 14 who takes the prize, for her pleated skirt and pineapple-leaf bodice, her slice-of-watermelon hat, the dangling bunches of grapes she wears as earrings. The decision of the judges— a distinguished panel including Jean Paul Gaultier, Boy George, a local drag celebrity called Tasty Tim, and a Brazilian pop star by the name of Fabio—is unanimous.

In other cases, the theme appears to have been a mere point of departure, from which some people have strayed such a long way that it is nearly impossible to retrace the path of their thinking: the guy with his hair in a crew cut, wearing a white babydoll dress and black Doc Martens, for instance, or the woman dressed in a sheath of American Express cards held together with metal links. There are three Madonnas, who may or may not be in Carnaval attire. The crowd parts for the reigning Alternative Miss World, a guy named Bruno—a mermaid with a paunch. The corsets that Vivienne Westwood has shown in her most recent collections—the kind that push your breasts up under your chin—are making a strong showing, on men and women alike. The music runs the gamut from house to disco to, on this particular occasion, samba. There are three deejays: one, a man who has come as Naomi Campbell; the other two, women, who often work topless.

Gerlinda says that she and Michael started Kinky Gerlinky in 1989 because they were "desperate to dress up." Born and raised in Regensburg, near Munich, Gerlinda had come to London in 1970 to learn English, after having completed her fashion studies in Paris; she met Michael and stayed on. Together, they went into business, opening a shop called World, which sells the sort of clothes that the people who come to their club nights might wear by day.

Now that Kinky Gerlinky has become something of a cultural institution, Gerlinda is regularly interviewed for magazines and newspapers as far-flung as the *Bangkok Post*. TV crews roam the crowd. Once a year, Kinky Gerlinky becomes an AIDS benefit, for which Gerlinda recruits big stars: Sinéad O'Connor, Boy George, Nick Cave, Neneh Cherry. People talk about Kinky nights in reverent tones, as a kind of forum for creative talents from the worlds of fashion and art and music and video. Lucien Freud, the painter, turns out on occasion to admire David Cabaret's latest incarnation-for-an-evening. David Cabaret has appeared as famous paintings by Roy Lichtenstein, Otto Dix, Andy Warhol; to enhance the effect, he carries a frame. His now-legendary version of Marilyn Monroe, who has become something of a drag stock figure, was as Warhol painted her: one side of his face hot pink, the other orange.

An inventory of the all-time great Kinky costumes would necessarily include David Cabaret's and several by Sheila Tequila, a.k.a. Sam. Sheila is as striking as Sam is unprepossessing. Where she commands attention, he's the first to admit that he's the sort of guy most people would never look at twice. He lives with his parents in the north of London. He has been doing drag for a little over ten years, since he was nineteen, and it is by far the most picturesque aspect of his existence.

Paging through his scrapbook, Sam recapitulates some of Sheila's finest efforts. There was, he fondly recalls, "Rich Bitch Goes Shopping," for which she sported a Christian Lacroix suit with a fox collar and a black crocodile Kelly bag from Hermès—both on loan, he hastens to add. "Jayne Mansfield Goes Jogging," in Reeboks, a turquoise jogging suit, and a silver lamé tank top, with a platinum-blond wig. "The Pakistani Stewardess," inspired by a Pakistan International Airlines tote bag found in a thrift shop: she wore a green sari and carried a rubber tube from a vacuum cleaner as a prop for demonstrating the use of the emergency oxygen supply in the event of a sudden change in cabin pressure. And—a resoundingly popular favorite—"Joan and Christina Crawford Go on a Picnic," for which Sam and his friend Donald dressed in forties-style mother-daughter gingham dresses. Donald, as Joan, with a ferocious mouth drawn in red lipstick, wore a huge sunhat; Sam, as Christina, in bobby socks and sandals, carried a little doll in a basket. Out on the dance floor, as bodies writhed around them, they spread a checkered tablecloth and unpacked their picnic hamper filled with sandwiches and cakes they had spent the whole day making.

"I really enjoy doing character looks," Sam says. "Most guys who get done up in drag, they want to make themselves look pretty. But I don't care. For me, it's more interesting to pick a theme and try and dress around that." He speaks admiringly of a drag queen he saw at a recent Kinky evening, wearing a Chanel scarf and a designer suit; when eventually the time came to fix her face, she opened her evening bag and took out a Christian Dior lipstick. "That was a nice touch," Sam says, "the expensive makeup." He has even, on occasion, done male characters, venturing farther afield. Once, he went to a club opening as a Los Angeles rocker—"a Guns N' Roses look," he says—in black leather and a greased-down red wig, and then spent ten minutes persuading the management that he really was Sheila Tequila, that he was harmless. To his mind, bad drag is, quite simply, drag that is uninspired—a cliché, like the *Cage aux Folles* showgirl look, which he finds obvious and old-fashioned. "I mean, it's a shame—a lot of people get stuck in a rut, thinking they've got to look glamorous. I'd rather just have a bit more fun with it, because there's so much more that you can do."

"Fun," as it happens, is Gerlinda's entire objective. Despite the high-flown terms in which Kinky Gerlinky's cultural significance is now discussed, Gerlinda still feels no great sense of responsibility other than that of showing her guests a good time. "I'm not serious about it," she maintains, "and I don't want to be serious about it."

On this particular occasion, for "Carnival in Rio," Sam has joined the multitude of Carmen Mirandas, though his conscientious attention to detail has once again set him apart from the rest: he has darkened his skin with body makeup. In the midst of his fellow Carmens, with their pasty-white complexions, he looks like a native among the tourists on the beach at Copacabana.

Upstairs, a peculiarly understated drag queen, respectably dressed, like a nice, middle-class housewife on a package tour to South America, is trying to convey what distinguishes her and her three friends from the drag rank and file. She goes by the name of Linda—just Linda, no last name, no play on words. When veterans of Kinky Gerlinky reminisce about the all-time great costumes that have gone down in memory, it isn't Linda and her friends that they recall. She is the kind of woman who would be kindly described as "plain." She prefers to be called "a transvestite," she says, quietly but firmly.

"We're trying to create a group of transvestites articulate enough to explain ourselves," she continues, "who can go anyplace and be accepted." Most recently, they have visited a popular wine bar in Mayfair and a quiet restaurant in Chelsea, both times without incident. Wherever they go, they proselytize in the name of drag, in the hope of opening people's minds—particularly the minds of people who might not otherwise come in contact with a man in a dress. At the wine bar, Linda says, "one guy was interested in finding out why we were doing this, but his mate thought we were chatting him up and pulled him away." She claims that there are a lot of new venues opening up for transvestites, thanks at least in part to the campaign she and her friends have mounted. They have never been hassled. "The feminine image is so powerful," she contends, the awe in her voice mingling with a certain pride, "that even when people know they're talking to men, they react to us as women."

Linda is on the verge of forty, and already she is anticipating the day when, like most women, she will have to tone down her makeup. "It takes a young face to wear really bold color," she laments. Like Sheila, Linda has been dressing in drag since her late teens; like Sheila, she has documented her best incarnations in a scrapbook, which, she says, she looks forward to showing her grandchildren. She had a girlfriend once, she confides, for whom she gave up dressing in drag, but after a few years they broke up, and Linda resumed what she regards as her pastime. She and the ex-girlfriend are still on good terms, however, and not long ago Linda took her along to Madame Jo-Jo's, a club in a basement in Soho, where a good proportion of the clientele was in drag. "She couldn't tell who was a man and who was a woman," Linda says triumphantly.

Asked the difference between a drag queen and a transvestite, Linda explains that a drag queen is more exaggerated and, frankly, gay. On the one hand, there's the Kinky crowd, which she and her friends consider "over the top." On the other, there's the Beaumont Society—explicitly heterosexual—which organizes weekend retreats, tea dances, and other get-togethers for transvestites and even support groups for the members' wives. Linda and her friends pride themselves on having more style than the Beaumont types they have seen pictured in magazines, in articles about the Society. Besides, she says, the Beaumont philosophy strikes them as "isolationist," intent on solidarity to the exclusion of the rest of the world.

Linda contends that the vast majority of transvestites are heterosexual—a belief cherished by members of the Beaumont Society as well, despite substantial evidence to the contrary. Drag queens make fun of women, she argues (in fact, many drag queens will go so far as to admit that drag is often misogynistic, but, like Linda, most of them are convinced that it is drag as practiced by other people that is pejorative). In contrast, Linda explains, when she and her friends dress up, the impulse is more along the lines of an inordinate *sympathy* for women—for what it's like to go through life as a member of "the tender sex," as she so sentimentally puts it. Still, they are quick to add, they wouldn't want to *be* women. Being a woman is labor-intensive and time-consuming, if you're serious about it.

One or two nights a week is plenty. Tomorrow evening, for instance, Linda will revert to being Stuart, who will play on the company cricket team and go out drinking after the match. Suppose her endeavors to make drag more widely accepted eventually succeed: Would she want her colleagues at work to be let in on her secret? "I think actually if it was totally accepted by everybody, it wouldn't be so wonderful," she concedes. "The 'forbidden fruit' aspect of it would be gone, which is part of the thrill—the idea of doing something a little bit naughty. If all my family knew, all my friends, everybody at the office, I would still do it, but it wouldn't be as much fun."

The taboo is intact, but the potential for scandal is in fact rather meager; the English are not so easily outraged by drag, unless there's sex involved. The average English person's first exposure to drag is early and benign, and it takes place under the protective auspices of the school, where annual plays in the panto tradition feature a principal boy, played by a girl, and a jolly dame, played by a boy. Onstage, drag becomes one of many theatrical conventions, perfectly acceptable. Barry Humphries, in the person of Dame Edna Everage, plays to sellout audiences; a suburban Australian housewife, she is beloved by everyone from the Queen Mother to Bob Geldof. Hinge & Bracket, a popular act consisting of two drag dowagers with a repertoire of patter songs, have been among the "mystery guests" who put in a surprise appearance as entertainers during the party scene in *Die Fledermaus,* for the annual New Year's Eve performance at Covent Garden; they tour the seaside towns, playing to their avid fans who live in the local retirement communities—a following that consists primarily of the very people they are sending up. A certain childlike innocence pervades the mass fascination with this kind of drag. The same innocence can also be discerned in the drag of various members of the crowd at Kinky Gerlinky: mainstream types from the outskirts of London, young couples out on a date, who have come dressed in each other's clothes because they've heard that that's what people do in the hippest clubs in Soho.

Predictably, perhaps, many drag veterans greet the arrival of these newcomers with a quiet resentment. Their drag is regarded as spurious; their eagerness, as suspect; their enthusiasm, as superficial and trendy. Their presence here this evening is something to be endured. Wait a year or so, and they'll move on, leaving the drag scene to the diehards. For now, however, the population of the dance floor is swollen with these dilettantes who converge like heat-seeking missiles on the latest London nightspot. Meanwhile, the target keeps moving, in order to protect itself—its refinement and sophistication, its exclusivity, its marginality. The process is always the same: the gay crowd initiates something, then the straight people come along and imitate it, watering it down until finally it becomes popular and commonplace. By which time the pioneers have gone on to something else, being obliged to stay one step ahead of the culture that, for all its aversion to homosexuality, doggedly follows wherever they lead.

Not everyone who comes to Kinky Gerlinky comes in drag. Drag is optional, but a head count conducted from the vantage of the balcony indicated that for every ten people, some seven were in drag. The other three, more often than not, were women, like the one with a shaved head, wearing a sheer black-mesh halter top, a dog collar, a garter belt, black stockings, and black leather military boots, or the one in a leaf-printed one-piece bathing suit with a white rubber bathing cap and fuchsia evening gloves. Men and women alike seemed to prefer to dress as women, although the women portrayed by the *women* tended to be far more eccentric and perplexing.

One of several Marilyn Monroes, none of whom have made the slightest concession to the evening's theme, is holding court on the stairs until a song with a thumping disco beat comes on, and then her audience disperses. She introduces herself as Candy Floss, heir to the mantle of Candy Darling, the famous drag queen who was part of Andy Warhol's circle. "I'm what Candy Darling would have been if she weren't dead," she declares. Two years ago, she moved from Manchester, her hometown, to London, and she has come to every Kinky Gerlinky since. But lately, she claims, she's grown a bit tired of the scene. "I went back to Manchester in drag, and they loved me," she says. "In London there are too many people."

....

The drag community in London is a fractious one, made up of several factions, which these days rarely overlap. What they share is a tendency to think of their own drag as the one true drag. Not all that long ago, back before there were so many venues for drag, these groups were thrown together on a regular basis at the drag balls at Porchester Hall, in Bayswater. But then the leather-and-rubber crowd swarmed the place and the whole atmosphere changed, with the fetishists outnumbering everybody else: by the time the local council moved in and abolished the evenings, the drag queens had already moved out.

Since then, they've gone their separate ways. Their attitudes toward one another are characterized, in varying degrees, by snobbery and condescension. The queens who worked the gay bars back when drag was part of a clandestine nightlife are suspicious of the public profile of the Kinky set; they talk wistfully about drag as a "tradition," its lore passed down from one generation to the next, and, like any elite whose long-term franchise is suddenly extended to the mainstream, they lament the ways in which drag is being "diluted" and "cheapened." The Beaumont Society "transvestites," who are adamantly heterosexual, regard those who are not, whom they call "drag queens," with disdain. The "drag queens," for their part, view the "transvestites" as unspeakably dowdy. And the avid clubgoers who have taken the amateur practice of drag to what is routinely proclaimed "another level" tend to see their drag as the creative culmination of what the others had been doing until they came along.

Although the drag queen who enters a gay bar in London no longer runs the risk of being harassed by macho guys who find the femme persona a disgrace, and although the members of the Beaumont Society have come out of the woodwork and declared themselves with pride, neither of these developments has done anything to change the nature of drag as practiced by these two contingents, both of which are—still—hermetic and self-contained. In purely esthetic terms, the real breakthrough has come with the Kinky Gerlinky school of drag, a groundswell that represents the confluence of London's somewhat rarefied art-and-design set with the popular culture of the seventies and early eighties.

Hamish Bowles, an editor at American *Vogue* since 1993 who previously lived in London and took an active interest in the drag culture there, traces the current renaissance to the so-called new romantic movement, which followed hard on the heels of punk. Punk, he says, had broken down the barriers that existed between what was possible and what was not. In its aftermath, the pillars of nightclub society were in search of something new—a look that would be less anarchic, perhaps, and not so unattractive. At Club for Heroes and the Blitz, they gathered, wearing clothes that were extravagantly historical, that drew on the styles of the eighteenth century, of England in the 1890s, of Weimar Germany, of thirties Hollywood; Bowles calls the references "multi-camp." As it happened, these developments coincided with a series of warehouse sales at Charles Fox, a big theatrical costume house that was going out of business. Bowles and his friends would go scavenging for bargains and come away with hats from the Ascot scene in *My Fair Lady*, bought for twenty pence.

It was a foppish period. "That was the first time you saw men wearing very heavy makeup," Bowles remembers. George O'Dowd, later Boy George, figured in these circles, as did Stephen Jones, one of London's most highly esteemed milliners. Culture Club, Boy George's band, gave this androgynous vogue a vaguely religious spin, and the imagery of their early videos influenced a wide audience of teenagers who were not privy to the arcane world of London nightlife.

In the clubs of the seventies, more often than not, the ambiance was overtly sexual and the objective was seduction. But as the awareness of AIDS set in, the mood changed, and a good time became not so much a matter of showing off your body as of dressing up and looking decorative. Bowles thinks that the shift was also the result of the political and economic context, a reaction to the grimness of Thatcherism. He recalls how Leigh Bowery, the performance artist who came to fame as a model for Lucien Freud's paintings, used to "adopt" kids he had met in the clubs, "secretary types" who would fall under his spell and reappear, transformed according to his whim into some character out of an Otto Dix painting. In those days, Bowles says, the dressing up was more "art statement" than drag.

By the end of the eighties, the night scene in London was riding an "acid house" wave, and the uniform for every rave seemed to be jeans and a T-shirt. And the raves were great, Gerlinda allows, but for anyone in search of an alternative, there was nothing. She and Michael would make regular trips to Rio, where they dressed to the nines, and to New York, to Susanne Bartsch's Fellini-esque club nights at the Copacabana, where their sartorial fantasies were given free rein. Finally, they agreed to produce a night in London, at a club called Legends, if only because it seemed so silly that they should have to go all the way to New York to dress up. The guest list was short, only three or four hundred people; in those early days, Kinky Gerlinky was like a private party. "We just wanted a place to go every so often," Gerlinda recalls. Maybe ten percent of the mailing list were not friends per se but friends of friends; the rest, she says, were people she and Michael knew—like-minded types who had grown bored with the drabness that had taken hold as part of the rave culture. They were encouraging: "Oh, we'll come in drag!" they would say. "We haven't done drag for a long time." Some of them, as it turned out, had never done it at all. And, according to Gerlinda, they looked "fantastic."

In no time, the word was out, and with every successive evening the crowd grew larger, until Legends could no longer contain it and it moved on to other venues: first, to the Café de Paris and, eventually, to the Empire Ballroom. Each time, Kinky Gerlinky had a theme, like "Label Queens," planned to coincide with the fashion shows in London. "Supermodel Divas" elicited hordes of Cindy Crawfords, with their penciled-on moles. The "vogueing" night, right after Madonna's "Vogue" video was released, was conceived as a joke, Gerlinda explains: "To do vogueing in England, it's like doing punk in Sweden. Because it's not our culture—it's Hispanic and black, it's a Harlem thing. So we decided to send it up." There was a contest—a distant echo of the one in Jennie Livingston's documentary film, *Paris Is Burning*—broken down into eight categories, including "Madonna Lookalike" and "Butch Queen, First Time in Drag."

....

"I admit, madame, or mademoiselle, I do not know what to call you, I admit that you are beautiful, but have you no shame at wearing such clothing and acting as a woman, seeing that you are fortunate enough not to be one? Go, go and hide yourself."

Monsieur de Montausier,
in *The Transvestite Memoirs
of the Abbé de Choisy*

Fairy tales and legends from sources as far-flung as India, Ireland, North America, and Oceania recount the fate of men who commit some crime against society and, in the service of justice, are transformed into women. Their masculinity is confiscated. Their freedom is curtailed, their rights revoked. If these cautionary stories are any indication, enforced femininity is, for a man, tantamount to a jail sentence, and the threat of it looms as a deterrent.

The practice of dressing boys in girls' clothes as a means of punishment seems to have taken hold in England in the second quarter of the nineteenth century, and firsthand accounts, as well as studies of more recent cases, testify to its devastating effects. Consistently, it seems, it is a woman—a mother, a maiden aunt, a grandmother, a foster parent—who dresses the child in drag, for any number of reasons cited again and again: disappointment at giving birth to a son after having longed for a daughter; the conviction that girls are more civilized than boys; fear and anxiety in the face of masculinity. And consistently, it seems, the child grows up isolated and resentful, incapable of identifying with either men or women, with a sense that his own personality has been thwarted. In modern terms, dressing a son in drag constitutes a subtle but severe form of child abuse.

A similar humiliation was apparently inflicted toward the end of the nineteenth century by wives who insisted that their husbands dress in drag—at a time when men's and women's clothes were as polarized as they have ever been, with women subdued by corsets and encaged in hoop skirts. In a debate that raged for years in the letters columns of Victorian newspapers, correspondents wrote of their own experiences with "tight-lacing," of the sensuous thrills it provided as well as the anatomical damage it induced. Husbands describe their marriages to women with the upper hand, who are older, or wealthier, or merely domineering by nature—women who have subjected them to a course in "figure training" every bit as rigorous as any that a girl might have been obliged to undergo, requiring them to wear corsets day and night, even while they sleep, and (in at least two instances) ultimately reducing their waists to a formidable nineteen inches. Those who rebelled were rewarded with a steel chain, fastened with a lock, that prevented their loosening the stays.

What was, of course, considered normal for women at the time takes on the horrific dimensions of sadism and torture when imposed on men. Their wives, however, seem to have regarded the enforced discipline as a way of evening the score. In a letter published in 1894 in *Society*, one reader, writing in the third person, explains his wife's attitude: "As he had at the outset expressed his desire that she should keep her own figure at the size to which it had been reduced, [she thought that] he ought to have some practical experience of the inconveniences attending such improvement upon Nature."

In the majority of these cases, it seems, the wives required their husbands to wear not only corsets but all the regulation trappings of femininity. The same man recounts that his wife has brought about a complete reversal, having commissioned for herself velvet knickerbockers and a matching jacket, fitted to show off her slender figure. While the women's clothes he is made to wear clearly demean the husband, a man's suit exalts his wife, enhancing the authority she already exercises.

Much of what transpired in these marriages seems to have been prompted, if not justified, by the wives' rage at the discomfort and inconvenience inflicted on them for the sake of fashion; dressing their husbands in women's clothes is their revenge. In another letter to *Society* in 1894, another miserable soul confides: "My imperious wife seems to delight in nothing more than the idea that she has forced one of the 'ugly' sex to conform to the dainty restraint of corsets, heels, and petticoats, which every pretty woman soon learns causes the helplessness that proves in the end to be her strength."

On a weeknight at Madame Jo-Jo's, in Soho, the entertainment is in drag, as are scattered members of the audience. The eponymous hostess sits, surveying the crowd. She is wearing a very proper black suit with a white collar, a triple-strand pearl choker and pearl earrings; her Chanel handbag rests on the bar in front of her. Half English, half Chinese, she speaks animatedly of her native Singapore, which she left over thirty years ago. She reminisces about Bugis Street, the heart of the city's red-light district, with its bars and its drag prostitutes: "The ladies of Bugis Street were the most beautiful creatures you've ever seen." Bugis Street, she says, was a training ground of sorts, setting the standard for a whole generation of drag queens and bar owners and nightclub impresarios; from there, they went out into the world. With a wave of her hand, she dismisses questions about what Bugis Street has since become. It's sanitized now—a tourist attraction, no longer worth the trip. Those were the days.

Madame Jo-Jo is matter-of-fact about her contribution to the local drag scene, which she sees as primarily a matter of marketing. Drag—good drag—existed in London in the mid-eighties, but, until she came along, it was relegated to the pubs. "We glamorized it and gave it a Continental feel," she says, and then it drew a different audience. While the drag bars feature female impersonators, Madame Jo-Jo presents drag entertainers in the "showgirl" vein. What she has in mind is more along the lines of the Crazy Horse Saloon in Paris: a good old burlesque revue with gorgeous girls in spangled bikinis and feather headdresses. If her cast on this particular evening falls somewhat short of that ideal, well, so does the cast of real women these days at the Crazy Horse. Nothing is what it used to be.

When the applause dies down, three drag queens at the bar lead the surge back onto the dance floor, a small area with flashing colored lights in the disco style. Their migration is ignored by five men in drag sitting quietly at a table in the far corner, talking in hushed tones, sipping the kind of drinks that women order—drinks that come in tall frosted glasses with slices of fruit straddling the rim. The members of this party are noteworthy chiefly because they are so inconspicuous—dressed in "neutral" colors, in blouses with padded shoulders and other clothes five to ten years out-of-date. Their wigs are cut and combed in a Princess Di blow-dry hairdo.

A maiden-aunt type, who introduces herself as Caroline, says that she and her friends work hard to strike "a subtle balance" in their drag: if they look too heterosexual, they spend the entire evening fighting off men on the make; if they look too gay, they feel out of place. They have never been to Kinky Gerlinky, which they consider "a bit downmarket." That's for "transvestites," Caroline explains, "which we're not—we're transsexuals."

She and her friends take great pains to make sure that the distinction is understood. "It's important not to mix us up with transvestites," Katerina says. "They are a totally different kind of people."

"I suffer them," Caroline continues, "but I prefer not to keep their company."

Like Caroline and the three other transsexuals with them this evening, Katerina has taken up residence here temporarily while undergoing the long process of counseling and hormone therapy that culminates in the sex-change operation. In time, she'll return to Germany, as Caroline will to South Africa. They are part of a sizable community of patients who have converged on London from all over the world, united by their common resolve to become women, drawn by the doctors specializing in cases like theirs and by the support groups. This is, they say, the best transsexual scene in all of Europe, even if their presence among so many other groups dressed in drag sometimes makes for confusion. In the evenings, they go out together and "practice" being women. And yet, despite the fact that for the time being their lives are built around a single, common objective, their rapport seems largely provisional; they have about them the edgy cordiality of strangers thrown together in a waiting room.

Their contempt for drag queens comes down to certain philosophical differences. "Our intention is to live in society as women," Katerina says.

"Actually," Caroline adds, "our goal is to disappear in society." Drag queens are, to their minds, appallingly exaggerated. "At all costs, they want to avoid being mistaken for a woman," Caroline explains. "So they let it be known that there's a man underneath that dress. There's a transvestite here tonight who's going around with two bottles of beer, one in each hand." She rolls her eyes. "I mean, that's a signal, and so *obvious*—that's his way of saying, 'Look here, I'm a bloke.' "

Few of the newcomers to Kinky Gerlinky have heard of Andrew Logan, but a good many of the longtime regulars recognize his Alternative Miss World competition as the forerunner of what Gerlinda's evenings have become. The catalogue for an exhibition of his work in 1991, at the Museum of Contemporary Art in Oxford, describes him as "moving between the fields of architecture (in which he qualified), decoration, sculpture, stage design and the organization of various 'alternative activities,' " including theater, opera, parades, festivals, and a beauty pageant of sorts: the Alternative Miss World. Logan inaugurated what has proved to be a hallowed, if sporadic, tradition with a party for a hundred friends in 1972, in Hackney, at the converted jigsaw factory that was his studio at the time. Billed as "A Surreal Art Event for All-Around Family Entertainment" and "a battle of poise, personality, and originality," the Alternative Miss World was, Logan explains, inspired not by the Miss World competition (as some might reasonably assume) but by Cruft's Dog Show.

The success of that first evening led to a series of others, at other venues: in a circus tent pitched on Clapham Common (in 1978); at the Academy, an old theater from the thirties, in Brixton (in 1985 and '86); in the Grand Hall at Olympia, an exhibition space for trade shows, where the runway was two hundred fifty feet long and the crowd numbered some twenty-five hundred (in 1981); at the Business Design Centre (in 1991). On various occasions, the panel of judges has included David Hockney, Ozzie Clark, Justin de Villeneuve, and Gerlinda, who, in 1975, rated a field of entrants that included one Miss Babylon—now her husband. Leigh Bowery, Susanne Bartsch, and Divine (a friend of Logan's, whose portrait he has painted twice,

PLATE 40

PLATE 41

PLATE 42

PLATE 43

PLATE 44

PLATE 45

PLATE 46

as a man and as a woman) have all been in attendance, at one time or another.

Contestants for the title of Miss Alternative World are evaluated in three categories—day wear, swimwear, and evening wear—as well as on the basis of an interview. The winner gets possession of the title, plus the Alternative Crown Jewels and the scepter, until Logan gets around to organizing the next event—which is to say, for one or several years. Many are called: among them Miss Wolverhampton Municipal Baths, Miss Tiffany Cartier, Miss Issippi, Miss Conception. Of the few who have been chosen to be Miss Alternative World, some have earned a place in the annals. "Drag" is perhaps too reductive a term to encompass the costumes of contestants who have come dressed as a creature or as a concept. An artist by the name of Bruce Lacey walked off with the crown in 1985, as Miss R.O.S.A. Bosom, a robot (her first name was short for Radio Operated Simulated Actress). The following year, Jenny Runacre, a real actress, took first place, as Miss National Geographic; for the evening-gown competition, she transformed herself into a volcano. Derek Jarman, the filmmaker, won in 1975 for his performance as Miss Crêpe Suzette, who gave her interview still trapped in the suit of armor she had modeled for the evening-wear portion of the program, playing her answers on a little tape machine.

As emcee, or, as he puts it, as "host and hostess," Logan appears split down the middle, with one side of his body dressed as a man and the other side as a woman—an idea that first came to him when he bought a half-and-half outfit in a "jumble sale" in 1964. In newspaper accounts, Logan, in his role as "host and hostess," has been described as a "transvestite," and he has replied with a letter to the editor. "Just to say that, in fact, I'm not. I told them that if I were, I wouldn't mind, but I'm not." Dressing in drag—the mere swapping of one gender for another—doesn't interest him; it's what he calls "the balance" that he finds so fascinating, the juxtaposition of both genders in a single individual, a single image. The makeup is confined to one side of his face; he applies false eyelashes to one eye. On one side he wears a woman's shoe and carries a handbag. The two halves of his body stand in different positions, make different gestures: the half of him that's a woman spends the whole night pushing the hair from a huge wig out of her face. Logan marvels at the extensive repertoire of hair gestures attributable to women. Based on his experience, he has concluded that most gender-related gestures come down to practical problems. And, he laughingly admits, women have a lot of practical problems.

Born in Whitney, a small town near Oxford, in 1945, Logan belongs to a generation of artists who have ventured far beyond the conventions of painting and sculpture. Critical opinion of the work he has shown in galleries—his field of giant stalks of wheat, surrounding and dwarfing the viewer, or his books studded with jewels and bits of broken mirrors—has been mixed. Respect runs considerably higher for the sets and costumes he has designed for the ballet. The overwhelming consensus is that the influence Logan exerts on the culture is at its greatest in the Alternative Miss World pageant. He considers the event "very much part of the sculpture" he does. Between these evenings and the rest of his work, there is a certain seamlessness of approach: he has been called "an artist of the school of Warhol and Walt Disney," which seems to please him.

Logan knows about Kinky Gerlinky, about its mainstream popularity, and he's all for it. "Because once drag becomes fashionable," he explains, "you get a lot of very straight people dressing up who would never have done it before. Which is great!" But Kinky Gerlinky is by nature commercial, and even if the spirit behind it is pretty much in keeping with the one that gave rise to the Alternative Miss World, Logan sees his mission as a different one, having to do with the values that underlie his making art. He believes that a large part of the Miss Alternative World pageant's impact resides in the notion that this is a rare event. "Doing it too many times would kill it," Logan says. He talks about the artists in India who make paintings out of rice powder as offerings to Krishna, which last for only a day, and he associates the Alternative Miss World with that sort of effort: a one-time "homage to people and to civilizations."

At Kinky Gerlinky, what started out as "art-statement" dressing escalated to full-blown drag (although the art statements continue). In London, as in New York, the cult of celebrity has infiltrated popular awareness to such an extent that the leading characters of the tabloid press are relentlessly imitated by drag queens. No one, it seems, escapes. People—or, more specifically, their appearances—become material suitable for comment, and drag, as it happens, is a convenient medium. On the dance floor at the Empire Ballroom, numerous incarnations of Elizabeth Hurley, Naomi Campbell, and Kylie Minogue, the minute Australian pop star, rub elbows with members of the royal family—Sarah Ferguson, Princess Di, the Queen Mum—in a hallucinatory version of what might otherwise be a swell party thrown by a very well connected hostess. Like a mirror reflecting Madonna's perpetual restlessness, there are drag queens who turn out as her latest persona, with the new hair style and color, the changes in makeup and clothes. They offer not so much the image of a woman as a visual proposition. "At the end of the day," Hamish Bowles says, "it's not even about looking like a woman—it's a completely abstracted notion, one that has nothing to do with what women really look like or who they are."

Most observers of the nightlife scene in London, Logan included, believe that what the local press has labeled the "drag boom" has been fueled by a certain subliminal discontent. The hunger for glamour, an eagerness to escape the confines of a humdrum life as the downtrodden foot soldier who goes off to a dull job every day, the nostalgia for another era, when women could devote more time and money to their looks, have all come together in the act of dressing up as somebody else. Many English fashion designers—among them Anthony Price, Rifat Ozbek, and, most notably, John Galliano—have taken an active interest in the ad-hoc outfits that turn up in the clubs, and to varying degrees their collections reflect it. French designers such as Jean Paul Gaultier, Thierry Mugler, and Gilles Dufour, Karl Lagerfeld's right hand at Chanel, have been known to cross the Channel for a look at the clothes in the clubs, convinced that these days that is where some of the most creative fashion happens. So a style born on a drag queen at Kinky Gerlinky might make its way—via the catwalks in Paris—to the pages of *Vogue*, where women will see it and adopt it. The notion of a woman looking to a drag queen's example for new techniques that might prove useful in the serious game of self-presentation is to some people's minds a disturbing one—as if real women ought to come by that knowledge naturally, when in fact women acquire it wherever they can find it. In magazines, in movies and on television, on the street and in their everyday encounters, most women are continually, however unconsciously, on the lookout for tips. A hairstyle, a way of wearing a belt or draping a stole—any visual information that could come in handy—is picked up and passed along, regardless of its pedigree.

At the bar at Madame Jo-Jo's, a woman in a Thierry Mugler suit with a cinched waist and a deep décolletage sat, fishing the olive out of her date's martini as he went off to make a phone call. Seated to her right, I struck up a conversation about the show and the drag scene in general. How would she feel, I asked, if she discovered that the suit she was wearing had been directly inspired by what some drag queen turned up in one night last year at Kinky Gerlinky? The suit clearly put her in mind of her own sex appeal. Would the knowledge that it was traceable back to a drag queen in any way diminish this acute sense of herself as a woman? "Oh, no," she replied instantly. Femininity, to her way of thinking, is a group effort, a collective endeavor. "Drag queens and women," she laughed, "we're all in it together."

ACHIEVEMENT

An impersonation is the supreme act of creation.

Yukio Mishima,
Forbidden Colors

....

At Wild Blue Yokohama, a recreational facility in the city for which it is named, a gigantic warehouse encloses a beach furnished with rubber-and-concrete sand, plastic palm trees, and machine-generated waves; the clientele consists of sunbathers, body surfers, and families on an afternoon's vacation, all of whom claim that they prefer this hothouse facsimile to the great outdoors because it delivers more of the essential experience of a day at the seashore than the seashore itself.

The artistry of imitation reaches its zenith in Japan, and the signs of it are everywhere: in the Tokyo Tower, a replica of the Eiffel Tower; in a facsimile of a Venetian canal (also in Tokyo), complete with gondolas, flanked by the facades of Italianate palazzi; in the karaoke bars, where yuppie businessmen practice their lip-synching skills on Friday nights after work; and, most recently, in the underclass of young Koreans who have styled themselves "the blacks" of Japanese culture, dressed in the manner of American rap artists.

Gaijin, or foreigners, may interpret this copycat urge as sheer greed, or as some form of cultural insecurity. They may see it as an affront, or as a lack of respect for the original, or as an almost fixational interest in a monument like the Eiffel Tower as a symbol—even a cliché—with no regard for its setting or its history or its context.

When Japan first adopted Western dress, during the Meiji era, it was not so much to mimic as "to absorb and master the new source of power," according to Liza Dalby, author of *Kimono: Fashioning Culture*. If putting on the trappings of another culture represents an attempt to enter into the alien sensibility that gave rise to it, to assimilate and surmount some outside influence, then drag might be one means of appropriating the power women have over men, the force of feminine attraction. The Zen archer's philosophy of becoming by doing, of approaching the inner state by going through the outward motions, seems to apply in Japan to femininity as well: it is a goal to be arrived at (by men, in some instances, as well as women) after long practice and preparation.

Some three hundred fifty years have passed since women were banned from the Kabuki stage and men assumed their roles. The *onnagata*, or actor specializing in female roles, had his counterparts in England, in the Elizabethan theater, and in Italy, in early opera; but in England and in Italy the convention died out. Performance styles evolved, naturalism took hold, and women were once again called upon to play themselves in a manner considered more true to life than any man's affectations. In Japan, however, the convention persists to this day, owing perhaps to the love of artifice and to the hallowed conviction that a woman—not any woman in particular but the essence of woman—may be better represented by a man. Yoshisawa Ayame, the great master of *onnagata* roles, who died in 1729, contended that a woman would be incapable of portraying the feminine ideal because her performance would inevitably fail to transcend the exploitation of her own features.

It is, then, hardly surprising that, over the course of the past fifteen or twenty years, surveys asking the Japanese public to name the personification of ideal beauty have often cited Miwa Akihiro, a drag diva whose career has included theater, films (most notably, *Black Lizard*), and cabaret. At Gin-Paris (*gin* in Japanese means silver), the Tokyo nightclub that she used to run, Miwa styled herself as part hostess, part chanteuse, surrounding herself with a decor reminiscent of Odilon Redon, rendering French songs from the thirties in Japanese translation for an audience of businessmen and their wives and a few fellow drag queens—all of them consistently moved to tears by her interpretation. On a call-in radio show, she would give advice to the lovelorn, who greatly valued her counsel, coming, as it did, from someone who knew the problems of both sexes firsthand. Gin-Paris has been closed since the end of 1990, but Miwa's celebrity continues. On the cover of a special issue of *Otoko*, a monthly men's fashion magazine, she is pictured in a dress of re-embroidered ecru lace, her Cher-like face framed by cascades of brunette, blond, lavender, and pale-blue ringlets.

Miwa's apotheosis is by no means an isolated instance; men in Japan have borne the burden of instruction in the craft of femininity for quite some time. The actors who took over female roles on the stage in the seventeenth century became the fashion trendsetters of their era, with women following their lead in matters of makeup and dress. In our time, *Elle Japon*, the Japanese edition of the French fashion magazine, has held up a handful of local drag queens as examples to its readers. "Their art of metamorphosis is so magnificent that in the end one understands why they criticize 'real' women," the magazine says, citing one young man who has taken to wearing spike heels around the house, to make his ankles more slender, and another who endured a corset for six months, to narrow his waist. "They monitor themselves constantly," the article marvels. "First, they turn their attention to their backs, so that they have beautiful posture. Then they must walk in an elegant fashion. Their Achilles heel is their hands, because plastic surgery cannot correct hands that are large. Consequently, they look for the best pose for their hands: how to arrange their fingers, how to put their hands on their knees when they're seated." These efforts are applauded, and female readers are urged to emulate the drag queen's assiduous self-refinement. "It's an attitude that is advisable for those of us who were born women. It resembles what one begins by adopting the uniform and the gear when one learns a sport."

One veteran Tokyo drag queen says that when he sees the way women on the street dress and apply their makeup, he is constantly tempted to take them aside and give them advice. In a society that prizes artifice in all things, it is perhaps inevitable that even masculinity and femininity would be viewed as artificial—arbitrary and not inherent, decreed by man and not by the gods (who in Japan are not much help in this regard, several of them being both male and female, or neither). The evidence of history suggests that, like the

French, the Japanese have felt compelled to improve upon nature: the tree is moved a few feet to the left; the rocks are placed in such a way that they redirect the course of the stream. Beauty in Japan is for the most part contrived: not a gift but an achievement, the result of re-arrangement.

A popular Sunday-night television program offers testimonials by men, some of them drag queens, and women eager to show off the results of their plastic surgery. Titled *Asakusabashi Yung Yohinten* (translation: "Asakusabashi Young Haberdashers," Asakusabashi being the name of a place, and titles in Japan being frequently baffling), the show documents the guests before and after their faces are transformed by more prominent chins, longer noses, creases in their eyelids. The so-called improvements in their appearance more often than not consist in "Westernizing" their features, and the fetishism that finds its object in noses and eyelids seems no less compelling—and a lot more widespread—than the fetishism that animates the pornographic comic books available at the local newsstand. In the work of Yasumasa Morimura, an artist living in Osaka, this distinction between Asian and Caucasian proves to be more intractable than the line that separates the masculine from the feminine.

The image is familiar—Manet's Olympia, reclining naked as, in the background, her maidservant brings her flowers from an admirer. But the details have been changed: the legs are muscular, the chest flat, the face that of Morimura, who re-creates famous paintings (many of them old art-historical chestnuts) with himself as one or several or all of the characters. As Manet's barmaid at the Folies Bergère, as both Judith and Holofernes as Cranach depicted them, with Judith wielding her sword in one hand and Holofernes's head in the other, as van Gogh's self-portrait, with a bandage on one ear, Morimura peers out at the viewer, his androgynous face taking on the expression of the original. He revisits Rembrandt's *Anatomy Lesson of Dr. Tulp*, assuming the roles of the teacher, the students, and the cadaver. Morimura has managed to step into the footprints of a wide variety of people who have gone down in art history's hall of fame—some well-known subjects, some anonymous painters' models, many of them so far removed from the experience and the appearance of a slight Japanese man in his forties, with a rather sad cast to his features, that there would seem to be no grounds for resemblance. The sight of him as a French woman is, as it turns out, no more incongruous than the sight of him as a Dutch man.

Critics, when they talk about his work, often resort to words like "appropriation," "simulation," "imitation"—words that Morimura finds unfortunate and misleading. He calls the art history that we acquire from books and lectures "knowledge," a prepackaged body of information and opinions. Morimura claims that he wants to think about art and its history in his own way, which does not come from the books. He is not trying to copy old paintings, he explains, but to carry on a conversation with them.

By means of photography, computer imaging, and an occasional application of paint or varnish to give the effect of brushstrokes, Morimura reproduces himself in various guises. Just as the trappings of femininity have belonged traditionally to women, the trappings of European culture have belonged to Caucasians. But now, as Morimura demonstrates in his work, both traditions are there for the taking, available for our consumption. Morimura contends that the things that constitute an indigenous Japanese culture—Shinto temples, for instance, or kimono or *ukiyo-e*—are in fact only a small part of Japanese culture as it exists today. When he thinks about living in Japan, he says, these things don't have much relevance. Like many Japanese, Morimura watches "foreign" movies, listens to "foreign" music, reads "foreign" books, and wears "foreign" clothes. His own education in art began with "foreign," that is, European painting and sculpture. This background, he maintains, has shaped his perceptions and determined his own personal "reality," and in his work he wants to use this reality as a point of departure.

Morimura defines his work as "a self-portrait." He continually depicts different characters, he explains, as a means for transforming himself, for changing both his body and his mind. With each new role he tries to experience something new, to discover something, to acquire something. He says that he thinks of himself as someone with the potential to be other than what he has been so far, and he sees his work as the occasion to explore these latent possibilities. The people we meet identify us according to our parents' name, our hometown, our nationality, our gender. Morimura concedes that these labels serve a constructive purpose, as everyday navigational aids that help us, as individuals, to get along in society. Even so, he resents what he calls the "limits" these labels impose, the way they hem us in at every turn, restricting our notion of who we are. He asks himself: Why must I be the child of my father and mother—why can't I pick my own parents? Why must I be "Japanese" just because I was born in Japan? Why must I be a man or a woman? Morimura describes his work as an attempt to transcend these limits. Experimenting on himself, he calls into question the identity assigned to him at birth, at random.

....

Terms like "drag queen" and "transvestite" have no precise equivalent in Japanese. *Onnagata*—literally, "incarnation of a woman"—is sometimes applied to a man dressed up as a woman at a nightclub or on the street, but more often, and more narrowly, it refers to professional actors on the stage—in Kabuki, for example. *Okama*, meaning effeminate (or gay, by implication), is pejorative, and patently offensive to many drag queens. The most recent entry in this category is a play on the expression used to describe the child of a mixed marriage—*hah-fu*, or "half" (one parent Japanese, one parent a foreigner). In a society that places such a premium on uniformity, *hah-fu* students are regarded by their one-hundred-percent-Japanese peers as anomalies at best, and as mutants at worst—half-breeds diluting the race. Lately, some young Japanese have taken to calling drag queens *nu hah-fu*, or "new half," to describe a hybrid of a different kind. Drag queens in Japan address one other as *hime*, or "princess."

The images of women that Japanese drag queens project often draw on two traditions that are seemingly at odds. There are the Western icons, selectively imported—sex kittens, like Marilyn Monroe, who is "immortal" (as opposed to Madonna, who is already "old-fashioned"), or tigers, like Cher; most drag queens in Tokyo, one party organizer explains, want to look "up-to-date." And then there are the deferential geishas, in native costume, mincing their gestures, their words, their steps. At Gold, one of the most popular clubs in Tokyo, where the theme parties on the first Sunday of the month draw a sizable contingent of local drag queens, a visitor can sit sipping a drink in the ancient-style tatami room and feel the floor pulsating with the bass vibrations of the music in the disco, down below.

It is impossible to dismiss the significance of drag in a society that has historically invested so much meaning in styles of dress. Clothes and identity are inextricable in Japan. During the Heian era, which lasted nearly four centuries, from 794 to 1185, men and women alike were subject to rigid sumptuary laws despite the fact that men went about their lives in public, in broad daylight, while women passed their days and nights in private, behind screens and thick silk hangings. There were regulations governing every last aspect of a person's outfit, right down to the number of folds in his or her fan: twenty-five for persons of the first three ranks; twenty-three for those of the fourth and the fifth; twelve for those of the sixth and lower.

Visitors to Japan today often remark on the availability of second-hand kimono at low prices; demand among the Japanese is nearly nonexistent, owing to the superstitious conviction that garments over time become imbued with the soul of the person who wears them. The conundrum, to the mind of a *gaijin*, lies in the fact that this society, which has consistently turned to matters of dress for making manifest the most subtle distinctions in class, would choose as its native costume the kimono—a garment that minimizes, if not disavows, any difference between the sexes. Even the customary Western practice of men's clothes wrapping in one direction (left over right) and women's wrapping in the opposite direction is without parallel in Japan; ever since the Yoro Clothing Code, an edict published in 718, all robes—men's and women's alike—have crossed left over right (the only exception being kimono for burial, which cross right over left).

Even so, Dalby notes, there is no mistaking men's kimono from women's; the differences, however slight, are clear. The men's kimono comes in drabber colors and smaller patterns. The women's is longer and worn bloused. The men's sleeves are sewn closed, while the women's are open from the underarm to the wrist. For men, the outside corner of the sleeve is square; for women, it is rounded. Even in modern Japan, in which the demarcation between male and female is far more sharply drawn, gender seems at times almost incidental, like an afterthought. The Mickey Bar, one of the trendiest restaurants of the eighties, in the Roppongi section of Tokyo, regularly featured a cast of Disney cartoon characters, including a woman dressed as Pluto and a man as Minnie Mouse.

A certain ambiguity pervades the language, as well. Waiters are *otoko-boi*, or "man-boy," while waitresses are called *onna-boi*, or "woman-boy." There is *tatemai* for what a person says, and *honne* for what he believes—a distinction that acknowledges and even condones the discrepancy between a person's innermost thoughts and the role he has been called upon to play (a discrepancy that in the West is called hypocrisy). The urge to pin down the ambiguities of human experience with either/or, black-or-white labels is not as strong in Japan as it is in Europe and America. Donald Richie, an American critic of Japanese films and a longtime resident of Tokyo, contends that "Asians in general, and the Japanese in particular, are not interested in the kind of polarities that create things like transvestism in the West." Masculinity and femininity are viewed as different, but they are not opposites.

As a result, the man dressed in drag does not lose his sex appeal for women. On the contrary, he may in fact find that his powers of attraction have been enhanced, even as he is accepted as one of the girls. Wakame, a drag nightclub performer, proudly numbers many women among his admirers. When his act is over, he joins them at their table. "Though I'm dressed as a woman," he says, "they find me virile. They find even that I'm more of a guy than their guys." Or perhaps he conforms more to their idea of what a man should be than the men in their lives. For several years running, an annual poll of Japanese women awarded the distinction of "sexiest male star" to Tomasaburo, the Kabuki *onnagata*, who appears in public as an androgyne dressed in a suit.

At Mandy's, a restaurant in Roppongi, the waiters are in kimono, dressed as women, with carefully applied makeup. Four Japanese O.L.s, or "office ladies," sit sipping their drinks, discussing different brands of mascara with the bartender, who prefers the waterproof variety, despite the fact that it's harder to remove. The women chat distractedly, their eyes following one of the waiters—their favorite—as he goes about taking orders, shuttling to and from the kitchen. These office ladies are his fan club.

Despite the presence of women in the contemporary workforce, feminism in Japan is something of a failed revolution, kept alive primarily by a handful of outspoken authors, most of them banished to academia. The confusion over sex roles and the sense of impending change that prevailed during the years prior to World War I—when "modern boys" and "modern girls" shared each other's clothes and cosmetics, when novelists wrote of emotionally fragile men and women who appeared in the street dressed in business suits and spectacles, when magazines regularly featured special symposia devoted to confusion over what came to be known as the "women's problem" (*fujin mondai*)—has long since abated. In its place has arisen a repertory of conventions, spelled out in the broadest terms in *manga*, or comic books for adults. Stock characters play out their readers' anxieties, with consequences that, however absurd or surprising, pose no threat to the status quo: protagonists like "Stupid Dad" on the one hand (a bumbling, ineffectual man, the laughingstock of his wife and children), or like "Rape Man" on the other (a heroic, Superman-like figure, naked from the waist down, with a perpetual erection as he flies to the rescue of innocent women and then, to their delight, assaults them). Sex in these tales is an escapade; women are simplified, reduced to their common denominator, like talking versions of "Dutch wives," the female dolls designed and marketed in Japan for use as sexual surrogates by men who are recently widowed or divorced or who find intercourse difficult. The victims in *manga* are unfailingly sympathetic to the problems of their aggressors, in keeping with what Ian Buruma calls a streak of "sentimental sadism" that runs throughout not only *manga* but pornography in Japan as well. If, as Camille Paglia has suggested, sentimentality and sadism are the caricatured extremes of femininity and masculinity in Western culture, then the Japanese have seemingly found one or several forms that combine them.

In Tokyo, in the area called Shinjuku, where the nightclubs are stacked one on top of the other, the newsstands are stocked with *manga* and magazines to suit every taste, however esoteric. *Samson* features explicit pictures of sumo wrestlers. *Queen* offers snapshots of transvestites in silky lingerie, lounging at home, or in evening dress, standing next to a stretch limo on a city street, or in prim suits, posed in front of a Shinto shrine. On the inside cover is an ad for Elizabeth's, a full-service drag club in Tokyo with a branch in Osaka.

Elizabeth's Tokyo headquarters is situated in Kameido, a few blocks' walk from the train tracks and a busy subway stop on a popular commuter route to the city's eastern suburbs. In business since 1979 (and in this particular location since 1988), the club attracts some twenty to thirty men on an average night, with the heaviest traffic just after office hours and only a few stragglers left by closing time, at ten P.M. The clientele, according to the manager on duty one Thursday evening, consists mostly of professional men—doctors, lawyers, businessmen, university professors—who drop by for a few hours on their way home to their families. The manager, an officious middle-aged woman wearing sensible shoes, proudly describes Elizabeth's as the only place in Tokyo where men can come and dress up and have their picture taken. On the first floor is a boutique selling clothes, makeup, and assorted drag paraphernalia; on the second, a suite of changing rooms and a bank of lockers; on the third, a lounge and a makeshift photo studio.

On this particular evening, business in the boutique is on the slow side. Everything a man needs to become a woman for a few hours is here: waist cinchers, earrings, foam-rubber falsies with erect nipples, girdles padded along the sides of the thighs and the top of the seat, comprehensive makeup kits that come in plastic carrying cases, like children's paintboxes. Lace-collared mauve polyester-crepe shirtwaist dresses and middy blouses with soutache trim vie for space with gold Lycra miniskirts and sequin-covered T-shirts. A late arrival carrying what looks like a gym bag over his shoulder drops in to buy some press-on nails and then proceeds upstairs. On the second floor, the shades are drawn. Under the glare of fluorescent lights, the men, in varying stages of deshabille, quietly go about the everyday rites of femininity. The vanity tables are scattered with makeup brushes, jars of cold cream, barrettes, eyelash curlers, and rotary electric razors. There are clothes to rent—most of them the sort of special-occasion dresses that women wear only once or twice. The cashier's desk is equipped with an electronic cash register and an abacus.

The music playing in the third-floor lounge is strictly easy listenin', a medley of fifteen-year-old pop songs rearranged for four-part harmonies and whooshing strings. The red-and-black indoor-outdoor carpeting, the silk flower arrangements, the velvet-covered sectional sofa, the trophies on a shelf, all put a foreign visitor more in mind of a midwestern American rec room than of a drag club in the Japanese capital. The beverage selection runs to coffee and tea—no alcohol. This is innocent fun, and nothing more. Men come here to try on women's roles along with women's clothes.

Back in the studio, a man in a print dress with a bow at the neck and a shag-cut wig is being photographed posing in front of a white seamless backdrop, one elbow resting on the top of a plaster column. The shutter clicks, the flash blazes, the film records the stance (self-conscious), the expression (coy), the outfit (leased). Just as the eye of the camera has habitually been trained on fashion models and debutantes and brides-to-be, the photographer here in this studio is preserving an image of womanhood in bloom, which is evanescent, even under the best of circumstances.

FUN OF FUTURE! the flyer exclaims. FICTO-FASHION-FIASCO! Diamonds Are Forever, a band of party-lovers who organize occasional club nights in Kyoto, is hosting its monthly extravaganza at the Metro, a cramped basement space with a bar and a few tiny tables and, at the far end, a platform stage flanked by potted palms. The entrance is a metal door on a landing halfway down the stairs to the Marutamachi subway station, Exit 2 of the Keihan railway. The decor is low-budget and vaguely in the Christmas spirit: red and green gels veiling the spotlights trained on the dance floor, a strand of little red lights encased in a clear plastic hose draped in swags along the iron railing. This is, however, not December but the end of April—the beginning of Golden Week, a stretch of public holidays that provides the year's best opportunity for an extended vacation. Kyoto, only two hours from Tokyo by the bullet train, is thronged with Japanese tourists, among them, several die-hard Tokyo club devotees who have come expressly for the occasion.

Every Diamonds Are Forever party is built around a theme. Tonight is Western Night. BOOTS AND SADDLE, RODEO EROTIKA, promises the flyer, along the bottom edge of which runs a lineup of wanted posters: mug shots of local drag queens, most of them Diamonds Are Forever veterans. The bounties on their heads range from "100,000,000$" for Simone F. to "2$" for Mamie to "−1,000,000$ (Includ TAX)" for Glorias. Just inside the entrance a local department store has set up a stand selling Stetsons, chambray cowboy shirts, and white lace prairie skirts, displayed on a folding table or hanging from nails in the wall, for the benefit of those whose costume is not quite complete upon arrival.

Apart from one or two *gaijin*, who are not in drag, the crowd is uniformly Japanese. At least half are men, bare-chested, wearing blue jeans and cowboy boots and ten-gallon hats. One shirtless desperado, whose eye makeup has been applied with a heavy hand, sports brown suede chaps over his Levi's and a fringed gold-leather neckerchief. Many of the young women have come in groups of three or four or five. In stretch minidresses and simple, high-heeled pumps, they look shy and adolescent and chaste, huddled together, whispering to one another as their eyes roam the dance floor. But they and the young men in jeans are eclipsed this evening by several dozen partygoers who have turned out in full frontier-girl regalia. In a few cases the inspiration is recognizable: Miss Kitty, Dale Evans. But for the most part the effect is slightly wide of the mark, with misplaced overtones of Mexico and Nashville.

The saloon girls are decked out in the latest underwear: spandex corselets and stretch-lace garter belts. A fat man's fleshy chest spills over the top of a flower-patterned bustier, bulging at the middle, where his waist should be; his thighs, in fishnet panty hose, are spindly, like bare wooden legs supporting an overstuffed chair. One "topless" cowgirl in fringed red-satin bikini briefs, stockings, and frilly garters, wears a pair of huge rubber bare breasts suspended from a halter around her neck. The drag is on the scale of a cartoon. Eyelashes are preposterously long and full. Mouths are enormous, drawn beyond the line of the lips and painted red. Wigs, framing unmistakably Japanese faces and covering straight black hair, are platinum blond and curly. Femininity as it is being exercised here this evening appears to be an outright refutation of nature.

By eleven-thirty, the dance floor is packed as tightly as a train at rush hour, a sea of heads and shoulders, all bobbing up and down in time to the music. There are no go-go boxes, but every so often, in a bid for the center of attention, a drag queen climbs up on top of a chair and dances. The lights aren't synchronized, the way they are in the fancy clubs in Tokyo; here, they rotate and blink at intervals, punctuated by the strobelike pop of flash bulbs as the Wild Westerners pull sleek cameras out of their pockets and take pictures of one another. The dancing is mostly polite and restrained, the movements small and close to the body. One European—a tall, bald, wiry man with glasses—seems to inhabit a space of his own, a red spotlight he fills with gestures that look like a cross between tai chi and vogueing; the crowd gives him a wide berth. The deejay plays a mix of disco and house, interrupted occasionally by tinny recordings of cowboy songs

("Tie yie yippy yippy yay") and a stern male voice announcing, in English, "This is a test of the emergency broadcasting system." A man in jeans, a T-shirt, and a sombrero threads his way through the mass of bodies, plugging one ear with his finger and talking into a portable phone. Every five minutes or so, a cowgirl toting a yellow plastic water pistol full of vodka shoots herself in the mouth.

At midnight, the entertainment begins—a drag talent show of sorts with acts that run the gamut from the innocuous to the bewildering. The mob on the dance floor obediently hunkers down and falls respectfully silent. The opening number is a concert version of "When Will I See You Again?" by the Three Degrees, lip-synched half a beat behind by a trio in bouffant wigs and long sheaths slit to the thigh, exposing the control tops of their polka-dot panty hose. Sexual symbolism seems to go over big. Bananas are peeled and eaten; guns are drawn. The warmest ovation goes to a solo performer wearing a pink pageboy wig, a block-printed silk dress, and silver gauntlets. She mouths the words to a Japanese rock song, reaching up under her dress when she comes to the guitar riff and taking out a loaf of French bread, which she mimes playing—first as a guitar, then as a keyboard. For the last chorus, she uses the baguette as a microphone and, in the heat of the final chords, breaks it in two over her knee and tosses the halves into the audience. Wild cheers ensue. A medley that includes "Buffalo Girls," "Dixieland," and the "Battle Hymn of the Republic" winds up the show, and the cast, inexplicably, brings out a naked department-store mannequin, dresses her up in a fringed bikini with a white mohair shawl draped over her shoulders, and sets her down on the dance floor, at which mysterious signal the audience rises and resumes its bobbing in rhythm, to an Annie Lennox song.

There are two kinds of drag, Emi Murakami explains: "The ones like us, and the ones who want to be real." A tiny woman with cropped hair and a warm, shy smile, she has been organizing Diamonds Are Forever club nights since 1989, not only in Kyoto but in Osaka, Kobe, and Nagoya, as well.

For breakfast, at five A.M. at the Coffee Tanaka, a twenty-four-hour coffee shop, Emi has changed into a hot-pink body suit and black pants. She and her cohorts discuss their philosophy of drag. There are, they concede, many drag queens in Japan who look just like real women. The so-called hostess clubs in Tokyo's Ginza district are full of them—men impeccably dressed in kimono, skilled in graceful movement and the art of demure conversation. Some of them, says Teiji Furuhashi, a.k.a. Glorias, the Diamonds deejay, "are even more perfect than real girls in America, because Japanese men are small and have no body hair." These male geishas entertain mostly business executives, serving them high-priced champagne and chatting about topics that take their minds off their work; meanwhile, the clients have the chance to exercise their connoisseurship of femininity, marveling at the flawlessness of their hostess's performance. But, Emi says, "we don't consider that good drag, because serious drag queens are not fun to look at." She and the others who participate in Diamonds nights on a regular basis call the kind of drag they do "party drag"; it is, they say, more "artistic" than "realistic." They agree that the ambition to look like a real woman is "old-fashioned," and they admit that they look down on that kind of drag queen, that they would never accept her as "one of the boys."

On this particular occasion, the Diamonds crew consists of a painter, a graphic designer, a dressmaker, a composer, a model, a self-described "visual artist," several "performance artists," a dancer, and a writer. On any given night, it comprises some fifteen or twenty people, most of them from Osaka, Kobe, and Kyoto, several of them members of a highly acclaimed avant-garde theater troupe called Dumb Type, one of them an American émigré from Detroit, all of them friends. Organizing these parties is "not really work," they insist. They do it for fun. "If you make any money on Diamonds night," Emi says, "you spend it on your costume the next time." "Most of us are artists," the American explains, "so for us this is a way of blowing off frustration." Like theater, they agree, drag gives people the chance to adopt another identity, a stage personality, if only for the space of an evening, so that they can do all kinds of things they would never dream of doing otherwise.

The kind of drag that the Diamonds queens practice seems more intent on approximating the West (America, in particular) and some attendant notion of what it means to be with-it than on conjuring any image of women in general. The demographics of drag are different in Japan, the Diamonds queens contend. Young Japanese men and women go to the States, they explain, where the most fun discos are the gay discos, and when they return home they re-create what they've seen: the break dancing and the vogueing, the hip-hop clothes, the drag. Teiji Furuhashi, one of the members of Dumb Type, has lived in New York, where he first dressed in drag in 1985 to go to the Pyramid club. "People appreciated drag queens there," he says.

Drag has become so trendy in Japan, Teiji says, that straight boys go out dancing in a dress (something he is quite sure that American boys would never do) because they want to look like the people they've seen in New York nightclubs. Teiji contends that Japanese gay people are in general "not as flamboyant" as their counterparts in Europe and America. In a mixed crowd in Japan, he explains, it's the wallflowers who are gay and the people bumping and grinding who are straight. In any event, the Diamonds queens agree, no one knows "who or what" most of the people who come to Diamonds nights are. The object is to have a good time. In Osaka, Emi says, the crowd really gets into the spirit, and everyone dresses up more. In Kyoto, there is always a contingent of customers who prefer to play it safe, turning up in their Armani jackets and their Chanel suits, although Emi and Teiji and their accomplices have been doing their best to discourage this sort of attitude.

To the extent that the Diamonds drag queens pay attention to fashion, it's as a source of ideas, none of which they take at face value. Emi and Teiji and their friends make their own costumes. They look at fashion magazines, they say, with a critical eye, always wondering what they can do to the outfit in the picture to make some sort of comment on it, to "make people scream." Their favorite designer is Thierry Mugler, with Christian Lacroix and Yves Saint Laurent tied for second. Something in the way Lacroix presents his clothes, what one of the Diamonds members calls "his sense of tackiness," leads them to believe that, in Teiji's words, he must be "a drag queen at heart," which is intended as a compliment.

If the age-old theatrical tradition of female impersonation in Japan represents men's idea of women, then the women in Japan have in this century been granted equal time, in the Takarazuka Young Girls Opera Company, in which the male roles are played by actresses who incarnate men as women would like them to be—particularly the women in the audience, which is made up mostly of housewives and teenage girls. Founded in 1914, in a climate of the Taisho preoccupation with androgyny, Takarazuka became a vehicle for female stars who "established themselves as the Clark Gables and Gary Coopers of Japan," in the words of Donald Roden, author of *Taisho Culture and the Problem of Gender Ambivalence.* The Takarazuka repertory is by now as codified as the Kabuki, the choreography and staging passed down from one generation of performers to the next. Buruma notes that many of the poses the male characters now assume were in fact copied from Marlon Brando movies. Despite these overtones of nineteen-fifties American machismo, the Takarazuka ideal is consistent with the fantasies of Japanese women who, when polled, say that the number one trait they're looking for in a man is tenderness. The stoic demeanor of the Japanese breadwinner, oblivious to the emotional life of his wife and children, is lately being called into question as women assert themselves. In 1989, Keiko Higuchi, a prominent feminist and author of *Bringing Up Girls,* founded her Hanamuko Gakko, the "School for Bridegrooms," in Tokyo, in order to instruct Japanese men in the ways of sensitivity.

That men, too, have found the centuries-old role in which they have been cast constraining, inimical to their own fulfillment, has gradually become apparent, though their protests are for the most part on an individual scale and, by and large, a cry not for the overthrow of the system but for greater freedom of expression within the system as it stands. *L'Homme geisha,* a French TV documentary aired in 1993 about transvestites in Japan, features Kageki Shimoda, a novelist who has become something of a celebrity, discussing his philosophy of outfitting himself in men's and women's clothes, all mixed together. "I am only trying to express my own personality," he explained. "What I wear expresses who I am, that which is deep inside me. The human being is not masculine or feminine, it is both at the same time." Shimoda is shown at home, drinking his morning tea, which is served by his wife. The cup he drinks from is larger than hers, according to standard Japanese practice. "I'm going to shave," he announces. "I'll prepare the bathroom," his wife replies. "What would you like to wear today?" she asks. He decides on the white sequined top. She helps him get dressed, in the sequined top, purple stockings, a miniskirt, rings, a poncho. The free-thinking advocate of sartorial change is, in keeping with time-honored tradition, patiently waited on by his wife.

The picture of businessmen whiling away the cocktail hour in the thrall of a transvestite geisha while their wives are busy swooning over pictures of the (female) hero in the Takarazuka program, a souvenir of that day's matinee, is curiously symmetrical, with each sex preferring its image of the other to the actual fact. But it is not a picture large enough to accommodate the Diamonds drag queens, who project an image of woman several times removed from the ideal at the heart of it—an ideal that, in any case, had its origins in some other, faraway society. The reverence that informs the geisha's every gesture, a literal transcription of some agreed-upon femininity, is conspicuously absent from the Diamonds queens' approach. Drag, they believe, should go "beyond" reality; it should be a "parody" of womanhood; it should be *naki ganai*—something to scream about. Roughly a third of the Diamonds drag queens are, as it happens, women: if femininity is a role (and a frequently comic one, at that), there is no reason why women can't play the part too. Over breakfast at the Coffee Tanaka, it emerges that the previous night's topless cowgirl is in fact a woman; concealed inside the gigantic rubber breasts were her own, which, she says with a laugh, are considerably smaller.

Growing nostalgic, the Diamonds queens reminisce about some of the all-time great Diamonds nights: Barbarella Night, Supermodel Night, James Bond Girl Night. Emi says that the themes always have to do with some Japanese fantasy, and that her only criterion is that they should be "obnoxious in some way and culturally relevant." The Diamonds cast has on various occasions included a Marilyn Monroe, a Barbra Streisand, a Julie Andrews (in *The Sound of Music*), and an Olivia Newton-John, as well as a Diana Ross and a Lionel Ritchie, who "sang" a duet. These were loose interpretations, along the lines of last night's performance by the ersatz Three Degrees. None of the Diamonds queens ever saw the Three Degrees. Imitating the Three Degrees, they maintain, is even better if you've never seen them, and better yet if you're imitating someone else who is imitating the original—like the kids in Japanese clubs who copy the moves in Madonna's "Vogue" video, which in turn copied the moves of the voguers in the clubs in New York.

In the hands of the Diamonds drag queens, imitation is elevated to an art form, one that takes other works of art as its raw material. Like the photographic "paintings" of Yasumasa Morimura (with whom Teiji studied at Kyoto University of the Arts), Diamonds drag comes to terms with a tradition by appropriating it. If some of the meaning gets lost in the process, so much the better. During the early years of the Meiji era, when the Japanese first took to wearing Western clothes in an effort to prove themselves equal to the European societies with which they were suddenly dealing, the men on the streets of Tokyo sported plaid shawls over their business suits; the idea of a shawl had been imported, but the fact that it was a women's garment had somehow been left behind. Such "mistakes" are unavoidable. The consensus among the Diamonds queens is that the more esoteric the original source, the shallower and more interesting the outcome.

ACCEPTANCE

Girls will be boys and boys will be girls,
It's a mixed up, muddled up, shook up world.

THE KINKS,
"Lola"

....

Margreet Esther Dolman began her career in the late seventies by doing interviews for a radio station in Amsterdam. She would pose offbeat questions in a somewhat hoarse contralto, and, in the final few minutes of the show, she would call her mother on the air and ask her what she had thought of it. Listeners would write in, asking for advice about their lives, most of them never realizing that she was a man.

It was just a matter of time before Margreet moved on to television, where her fans at last laid eyes on a solidly built blonde with a square jaw and earnest brown eyes. She dresses in a matronly style, in pastel colors, mostly lavender and pink, and wears no makeup. Every Sunday, some three hundred thousand people tune in to *Paul Haenen vijf over zes* ("Five After Six"), the show on which she appears, named for the time when it airs. She also publishes a monthly magazine, *Margreet Dolman's Mens & Gevoelens* ("Humanity & Feelings"), which is sold by subscription and on newsstands all over Holland. The pages—a patchwork of poems, letters, essays, snapshots, and cartoons, some of them sexually explicit—have a homemade look to them, as if they'd been assembled on her kitchen table.

Paul Haenen is Margreet Dolman. He is also Zoals Gredaat, a bisexual priest who turns up on the show with his hair slicked back, wearing aviator sunglasses and a ski sweater. Haenen says that Margreet, like Zoals, is "part of myself," that playing a woman is second nature to him, although, he insists, he has no particular urge to wear a dress. Haenen uses his show to campaign for acceptance of all sorts of minorities, and uses Margreet in particular as a device to get certain points across more effectively than he could if he were to make them himself. In one episode, she comes upon two men in bed together, apologizes for the intrusion, and, in a motherly gesture, turns out the light on the nightstand. She also dispenses advice with an authority that Haenen, as himself, would probably lack. When a young Turkish girl sends a letter saying that her schoolmates call her all sorts of horrible names, Margreet reads it on the show and orders them to stop that.

Margreet Dolman may not typify the style of drag to be found in Amsterdam's clubs, but as it turns out she is a fairly good indicator of the extent to which drag in Holland is integrated into the popular culture. Both she and Francine, a.k.a. Frans Kubin, who holds court at a club called the Roxy, exude a coziness that is instantly endearing. Francine, however, is a glamour girl, with an arsenal of feather tops, sequined miniskirts, rhinestone tiaras. She is also heavyset. Among Francine's moments of glory was her appearance in a TV commercial for Croky Chips, a Dutch brand of potato chips. In spike heels, a long blond wig, and a red evening gown that hugged her every curve, she was handed a bag of Croky Chips, took one, pushed up her falsies, and passed the chips on. While many women would go on a diet or, at the very least, reproach themselves for being fat, Francine appears to be content with herself as she is. She's overweight, she says unapologetically, because she's a glutton, eating nonstop all day long. "But I'm not the chippy type," she explains, despite the nature of her career in commercials. "I'm more of a cheese-sandwich dame."

Francine's apartment is filled with pictures of herself, each one commemorating an outfit or an occasion. She looks to magazines, TV, and music videos for her fashion inspiration, she says; she cites Annie Lennox, in particular. Francine rarely buys her clothes off the rack: "Too common," she sniffs. She talks with disdain about the new generation of drag queens in Amsterdam—their hippie style, their slipshod hair and makeup. "They dress so *cheap*," she complains. "And you don't have to spend a lot of money to look nice. But they're *really* cheap—you know, they get a dress for one guilder from the flea market, and then they don't even wear any panties. And their hairy chests. . . ." Francine believes that if you dress in drag, you should look like a woman. And if you want to go no more than halfway, then don't even bother.

Emile, a friend of Francine's who is roughly the same age, in his thirties, says that the newcomers' forays into the drag scene in Amsterdam are too sporadic to be taken seriously. *His* generation, he says, was clubbing every weekend. Emile started doing drag in the late seventies—punk drag, as he defines it. It was only when, as a law student, he went to work part-time at Madame Arthur's, the Amsterdam branch of the Paris cabaret, that he made the transition to what he calls "beautiful" drag. Going on stage taught him a lot, he says, but the real incentive to improve his wigs and to refine his makeup came after the show, when, along with the other members of the cast, he was obliged to sit among the customers, drinking champagne and chatting with them, up close.

In drag, Emile goes by the name of Joke (pronounced Yo-ke), a common name in Holland—a name for a housewife, he explains, ironic in this case: the people Joke meets are always surprised to learn that such a bombshell isn't called something like "Chantal" or "Henriette." She started out as a blonde, then became a redhead, which she considers "more artistic." As a man, Emile wears stylish clothes, carefully considered and well put together. But when he dresses as a woman, his style is more haphazard—no designer labels (primarily because they don't come in sizes big enough to fit him), no matching shoes to coordinate with the dress. For him, drag represents a freedom from the rigors of good taste, which as a man he upholds continually, without respite.

Emile admits that the drag queens in Amsterdam are not as chic as the ones he's seen in Paris, nor are they so preoccupied with fashion trends. Still, Joke, like Francine, strives for beauty. Beauty is the object of the exercise. Fatzy Smith, otherwise known as Franck Wydebos, disagrees. "Beauty's not that important," she says. "It's more important to have good shoes, good panty hose, and a nice dress you can sit and walk in. Then comes the face." Black, born in Surinam, Fatzy came to Holland at the age of fourteen and began doing drag six years later; she's now in her thirties. Fatzy calls drag "my profession," and at this point in her life she doesn't even show up for a party unless she's paid. "People have this idea that a drag queen is something to laugh about," Fatzy says. "For me, what I'm doing is serious, and it's really hard work. I wish they paid me as much as they pay Tom Jones." Fatzy has studied acting and ballet; she performs in a cabaret. She even had her own television show, called *Fatzy & Co.*, but its run was brief because (this, now, is according to Francine) Fatzy couldn't ad-lib and keep up a running patter in front of the camera.

Fatzy, Joke, and Francine are all of the opinion that drag queens, like women, have to guard against becoming old-fashioned. Constant vigilance is required: attention to changes in fashion and in makeup, a dispassionate assessment of the face in the mirror. Old-fashioned is to their minds the worst thing that a drag queen can be. Joke contends that it creeps up on you, that it can happen to anyone. She wore the same Tina Turner–style wig for four years, long after Tina Turner and her wild-woman hair had gone into eclipse, until one day she realized that the times had changed and she'd been left behind. "That's the problem with old drag queens," she laments. "They think, 'Oh, this is the best look for me,' because that's the look they were doing when they were younger and everybody paid attention to them, and so they stay with it." Just as women do—as somebody's grandmother still wears her minidress from the sixties because that was her heyday. Francine has been to Zurich, where, she says, the drag queens were dowdy beyond belief: their hair was too big, their dresses too long. They looked exactly the way a dowdy woman looks—no difference. Joke says the most old-fashioned drag is the kind practiced by the queens who still perform. She used to perform but wouldn't dream of doing it now, because music has changed so drastically. "Drag queens need a singer to imitate," she says. "They can't do original material, because they need to lip-synch. With house music, electronic music, rap—there's nobody to imitate. Besides," she remarks, "there are no stars now—not in music, not in the movies." That's why, in her opinion, drag queens, when they go to impersonate somebody of our time, resort to fashion models, who are famously silent.

Francine says she has been to London and met transsexuals who complain that drag queens are too exaggerated, that they're making fun of women. "We're just trying to *be* women," they say, "we're trying to blend in. And all these drag queens are making fun of women."

But Francine has no compunctions about the way that she and her colleagues portray femininity. To her mind, they're aspiring to its acme: to womanhood at its finest. Let the transsexuals represent the average. Francine and her fellow drag queens will strive for the perfection that beauty contestants and Hollywood starlets have, to her mind, abdicated.

In fact, there are aspects of Francine's experience that bear an uncanny resemblance to the lives of many women. She registers some of the same discontent that outspoken women do, in private, among themselves. "Men!" she says. "Really, most of them don't have a lot to offer. I mean, they may be fine between the sheets, but then the mouth opens, and I think: *Pleeze*, out that door! *Now.*"

Emile, for his part, is convinced on the basis of his experience in drag that being a real woman, twenty-four hours a day, is no picnic. There was a time when he dressed as a woman, day and night; he was living in Paris, taking hormones; he had breasts. And men ogled him in the streets, he says. Now, however, he prefers to dress up, go out in drag, get lots of attention, then go home, take it all off, and be done with it. How tedious—how relentless—it must be, he imagines, to be a woman, someone who is looked at all the time.

But the spotlight for a drag queen in Amsterdam is, if anything, rather small and intermittent. Francine, Joke, and Fatzy all agree that the Dutch are so goddamned tolerant, not just of drag but of all kinds of behavior, that it's hard to get their attention sometimes. At It, one of Amsterdam's most popular clubs, a man dressed as a French maid from a Feydeau farce moves through the crowd on the dance floor—a remarkably homogeneous collection of young men in denim and leather, none of whom seem to notice the drag queen in their midst. At the Roxy, a man in a black bra and girdle, black evening gloves, pearls, and a blond wig is swanning around the bar, to no avail; more heads are turning for a pumped-up guy in a sheer stretch T-shirt. This is a city that has established a Prostitution Information Center in the middle of the red-light district, where the women display themselves, like merchandise, in storefront windows; in the coffee bars, marijuana is for sale. This is a country in which the television audience is treated weekly to a gay dating game, hosted by a drag queen, and, on a more occasional basis, to talk-show interviews with Maarten 't Hart, one of Holland's leading novelists, chatting nonchalantly in a wig and a dress. No one imagines that the Dutch are libertines themselves, or that they don't personally disapprove of men in dresses, to say nothing of other aberrant types who have made this city their home. But transgression is regarded as a highly individual matter and not the business of the society. The live-and-let-live school of thought prevails, for better or for worse.

For worse, Fatzy would say. "Here in Holland," she grumbles, "you look good, but so what?" The Dutch are accustomed to taking all things—even beauty—in stride. Besides, she claims, the everyday ostentation that sets the stage for good drag simply isn't a part of the everyday landscape in Amsterdam. She ticks off a list of what's missing: "There are no Rolls-Royces in the street, there is no Claude Montana boutique. . . ." And so on. "Everybody is so down-to-earth," she says glumly. "Not even the real women dress up here."

ALTERNATIVES

Cosmetics and the intricate cross-purposes of being a man and being a woman seemed to impel him forward, and he could look, at times, as if he were pressing his face against a pane of glass, speaking distinctly and a little too loud to someone on the other side.

MICHAEL CUNNINGHAM,
Flesh and Blood

The Fourth of July dawns muggy and overcast, and all along the south shore of Long Island people are turning on their radios, tuning in to the weather forecast, wondering whether to call off their barbecues and their softball games. In Cherry Grove, on Fire Island, preparations for the annual invasion of the Pines, a neighboring community, are proceeding according to plan, regardless. The *Fire Island Clipper*, a double-decker ferry, is docked at the pier, where a bearded nun wearing pink lipstick, a stainless steel and gold Rolex, and a habit that exposes a lot of chest hair is exhorting the passengers to hurry up and get on board. But the passengers are in no hurry. A red-wigged Eliza Doolittle pauses to soak up the applause from the crowd, modeling a painstaking reproduction of the black-and-white-striped satin dress and black-plumed picture hat that Cecil Beaton designed for Audrey Hepburn, for the Ascot scene in the film of *My Fair Lady*.

"Bless you, my child," the nun, who goes by the name of Pansy, tells a hefty brunette in fuchsia chiffon who takes after Liz Taylor in one of her fat phases. Pansy has participated in the invasion of the Pines since the beginning, in 1984, when a group of drag queens from Cherry Grove decided to band together and lay siege to the Pines, a homosexual enclave where the prevailing mode was macho and anything else was frowned upon.

A reasonably credible Marilyn Monroe, dressed in a draped orange chiffon evening gown, blows a stage kiss to her catcalling fans. "Step lively, girls!" Pansy calls through a battery-powered bullhorn. Once on board, the passengers go upstairs and position themselves conspicuously along the railing. The spectators on the pier gaze up at them, silhouetted against the hazy sky. A man in a lavender chiffon dress and a Miss Piggy mask arrives, escorted by a woman as Kermit the Frog. The valances of the red-and-white-striped awnings on the buildings that line the harbor flap in the breeze. Pansy shoos the last few latecomers on board, and then, when the captain sounds the horn, a cheer unites the passengers and the crowd, dockside, that has turned out for their send-off. The ferry pulls away; the bystanders, save for one, straggle back to the lazy business of a holiday afternoon. The bare-chested man left standing on the pier, outfitted in motorcycle boots, black leather shorts, and suspenders, grows smaller and smaller in the distance. As the boat rounds one of the arms of the harbor, he can still be seen—a figure in miniature, waving good-bye.

On the upper deck, where the wind is strong, a Mother of the Bride in mint-green satin clamps her pillbox hat to her head. A light rain has begun to fall, and one blonde wearing glasses and pearls and bright pink patches of rouge pulls a packet the size of a card case from her pocketbook and unfolds a fan-pleated plastic rainhat. "Sorry. Sorry," a redhead on her way toward the front of the boat apologizes in a heartfelt baritone every time her skirt, in tiers of pastel-colored tulle, gets caught on someone else's outfit. A squaw in a blond wig plays the accordion. A woman wearing a baseball uniform, its stripes stretched tight over her padded paunch, roams the deck, a bat and a glove in hand; her long sideburns are painted on. The passengers pull cameras out of their handbags and take pictures of one another, posed in groups of two and three against a backdrop of gray sky blending into gray water, the horizon a blur. Stray feathers, from boas that are molting, drift like fallen leaves across the floor, propelled by the breeze.

The boat passes a cabin cruiser inhabited by four men, sunbathing. "Hi, boys!" two good-time girls hanging over the railing call out in voices that lie squarely in the male register. Someone toward the back of the boat starts singing. "Stand beside her"—others join in—"and guide her"—as little by little the song gains momentum. "From the mountains—" Soon, everyone is singing. "To the prairies—" The words are sung with feeling. "To the oceans white with foam—" The rousing sound of the chorus is carried away on the wind. "God bless A-me-ri-ca, my home—sweet—home!"

Downstairs, Eliza Doolittle sits all alone, gazing out the window. Soon, the Pines hoves into view. Noses are powdered; lipstick is reapplied. Suddenly, the sound of the chatter and the motor and the waves is drowned out by the wailing of a siren as the ferry is intercepted by a speedboat with a flashing blue light and a stern-looking crew of three men in black T-shirts and white pleated shorts, clutching binoculars. FASHION POLICE, the boat says on the side. But no arrests are made. The fashion-police escort guides the ferry into the harbor, through the marina, past boats with names like *Carpe Diem* and *Obsession* and *Aquarius*, flying helium-filled silver Mylar balloons and little American flags. The dock is thronged with men, most of them in T-shirts and shorts. "We are so pleased to be with you today," Pansy tells them from the prow as the ferry is moored in front of Island Properties Real Estate. One by one, the passengers disembark and make their way along the pier, as if it were the catwalk for a fashion show. "C'mon ladies, step lively!" Pansy urges the ones who linger too long. "They've seen you. Now they want to see someone else."

The divas wait till last. Marilyn Monroe vamps for the crowd from the upper deck. She checks her reflection in the window of the boat's cabin, and primps. Finally, she makes her way down the stairs, pausing to rearrange her mouth before she steps off the boat, her features set in that look of perpetual surprise that was Monroe's trademark. Her breasts are less convincing: immovable, prosthetic, they stay firmly in place while the rest of her body writhes in slow motion.

On one of the boardwalks nearby, a group of weekend residents has gathered to watch the ongoing parade and review the invasion. "This was a particularly heinous year," a longtime veteran says, as facsimiles of Joan Collins and Linda Evans stump down the stairs leading to a popular restaurant's sundeck. "That wig," one aficionado says of Linda Evans's blond mop, which looks mangier as she gets closer, "is strictly for distance work." A debate about the merits of the Pines' own drag queens, dressed up in honor of the invasion, and those who have arrived by boat from Cherry Grove, comes down on the side of the Pines queens, who, it is decided, are more sophisticated and more creative. "Holy shit, there's my dermatologist!" a bystander exclaims as he spots a man in a curly red wig and an off-the-shoulder Lycra dress that rides up with every stride.

A photographer for one of the local papers has his camera trained on a blond-wigged giant who bears a remarkable resemblance to Claudia Schiffer, the Chanel model who, for her part, bears a remarkable resemblance to Brigitte Bardot. The Claudia Schiffer look-alike is surrounded by a corps de ballet of six, all of them dressed in a style in keeping with Karl Lagerfeld's latest collection for the house of Chanel—clothes for an antebellum motorcycle gang: big yellow tulle skirts and yellow-and-white gingham jackets, festooned with matching gingham camellias, quilted gingham bags, chain belts, drop earrings, bows, white organza picture hats, black biker's boots. Claudia Schiffer is escorted by a man in a contoured Azzedine Alaïa–style dress made entirely from pieced-together Fruit of the Loom white cotton-knit Y-front briefs. A rival team arrives, outfitted in dresses with scoop-neck bodices and full black point d'esprit skirts, wide-brimmed black straw hats, belts, and sunglasses. "They're Dior, we're Chanel," one of Claudia Schiffer's contingent announces.

"Honey," Michael Kors, the fashion designer, corrects her, "it ain't Dior—it's more like Anne Klein."

The sun has come out and burned off the haze, and the heat is stifling. "People's faces are melting," one observer remarks. The strapless dresses are slipping.

A dead ringer for Divine comes teetering along and gets her heel stuck in a crack in the boardwalk. "Enough of this boardwalk shit," she mutters. "Why can't this place get some sidewalks?"

"Wear flats!" a local resident snaps back.

"People use drag," one bystander says, thinking aloud, to his friends, "to release their anger? There's some kind of aggression going on here."

At the foot of the stairs stands a man wearing a white T-shirt and denim cutoffs over biker's shorts. He is holding a black Pekingese. "Nice dog!" Linda Evans barks as she stumps past.

The dog is wearing a bow. "Is it a boy in drag or a girl?" Eliza Doolittle asks shyly.

PLATE 47

PLATE 48

PLATE 49

PLATES 50, 51, 52, 53

PLATES 54, 55, 56, 57

PLATE 58

PLATE 59

PLATE 60

PLATE 61

PLATE 62

PLATE 63

PLATE 64

PLATE 65

PLATE 66

PLATE 67

PLATE 68

"It's a girl," the man replies, indignant. "I wouldn't do that to a male dog."

Why, as to those who diverted me from my troubles, I could name them thus and implore them from the depths of myself, "O monsters, do not leave me alone. . . . I do not confide in you except to tell you about my fear of being alone, you are the most human people I know, the most reassuring in the world. If I call you monsters, then what name can I give to the so-called normal conditions that were foisted upon me?

COLETTE,
The Pure and the Impure

Dubbed "the Queen of the Night," Susanne Bartsch is the first to admit that her empire isn't what it used to be, before she came to power, and that it's AIDS that has put a damper on the fun. Even so, although the prospect of spending the night with a stranger is now fraught with all kinds of qualifications, not everyone is staying home alone, and for many of those who do go out, the erotic adventures seem to be not sexual but sartorial. On the last Thursday of every month, at the Copacabana, the club on East Sixtieth Street, Bartsch plays hostess to her friends, who number in the hundreds, the vast majority of them determined to let loose for the space of a few hours all got up (a large percentage of them in drag) in outfits they have been working on for weeks.

"I'm sorry I have to charge you," she tells them, "but you understand." She really is, and they do—after all, she has to make a living. Even so, she manages to keep the price at the door to ten dollars, which is fairly reasonable when you consider what you're getting: two dance floors, musclemen, voguers, drag queens, to say nothing of Bartsch herself, presiding over events in some gala showgirl concoction that pushes up her breasts and cinches in her waist, and wearing her trademark platform shoes, false eyelashes, and, often, a wig that makes no attempt to pass itself off as human hair. Despite the Dionysian mayhem, Bartsch's parties are closer in spirit to Disneyland than to bathhouse orgies. Louis Canales, a publicity agent and club owner who has persuaded Bartsch to go to Miami and organize a monthly night there, characterizes the atmosphere as one of "naïve decadence." Marc Jacobs, the fashion designer and a friend of

Bartsch's, marvels at her seemingly indelible innocence. "She can talk about genitalia and having sex with sailors," he says, "and it doesn't seem dirty somehow."

A vixen with the heart of a Girl Scout, Bartsch is beloved by her friends, all of whom, either consciously or inadvertently, do impersonations of her Swiss-German accent, with its interchanged *v*'s and *w*'s, superimposed on a steady stream of Cockney turns of phrase. Her conversation is a constant source of entertainment. Nouns can become superlative adjectives, as in "a genius hairdo," or "That outfit is showtime!" Mostly because she can't remember people's names but also partly as a term of endearment, she calls everybody, regardless of sex or sexual preference, "girlfriend," the way someone of an older generation might call everybody "dear."

In January, a week before the club night in Miami, the scene in Bartsch's apartment, in the Chelsea Hotel, is one of happy, if way-out, domesticity. In the living room, painted an intense shade of pink, with fat pink and green swirls around a purple sunburst at the center of the ceiling, a hammer and screwdrivers lie scattered next to the fireplace, where her husband has been working, renovating the apartment. Susanne's Rolodexes are lined up on the table, by the phone. In the middle of the floor sits the vacuum cleaner. "Swiss foreplay," she explains.

A slender woman with long, dark, curly hair and bangs that obscure a lack of eyebrows, and with a pointy high-bridged nose and a mouth stained a medium red, Bartsch looks no more than two-thirds her age, which is close to forty. Because she has spent the afternoon calling on potential sponsors for the Love Ball, a benefit she is organizing for AIDS, she is wearing what she jokingly calls her "natural look": a Betsey Johnson jersey zip-front jacket, miniskirt, and leggings, all in a bright-colored print featuring the Statue of Liberty, roses, and hearts wrapped in banners emblazoned "MOM"; black Nike sneakers with two-inch black rubber platforms; and a duckbill cap covered with bright-colored sequins the size of Necco wafers. Her husband, Ty Bassett, who has pale-blue eyes and close-cut blond hair, looks barely twenty-three, which he is. They were married one afternoon in 1988, on a break from decorating a club called Bentley's, on East Fortieth Street, where Bartsch organized a weekly night.

If there's a theme that runs through the various jobs Bartsch has held, it is perhaps a fascination with the way people present themselves. She came to New York in 1981, by way of London, where she had gone at the age of sixteen to get out of Switzerland. Born and brought up in Bern, she comes from good, solid mountain stock; her parents were, by her own description, "the kind of people who went to school on skis." Her father was a flooring contractor. "Tiles and winyls," she says.

Bartsch rattled around London, knitting sweaters to order, working as a hairdresser's receptionist, running an antique-clothing stand in the Chelsea Market, eventually dealing in old jewelry and, she says, "bric-a-brac." In New York, she opened an eponymous shop in Soho, importing clothes and accessories by Body Map, Stephen Jones, Leigh Bowery, Andrew Logan, and other designers who were part of the highly volatile London fashion scene. But it wasn't until 1987, when—as a lark—she organized a night at a club called the Savage, that she found what many people consider to be her true calling. That evening was the first in what soon turned into a weekly tradition. John Badum, an executive for a sportswear company and a friend of Bartsch's, says that the Savage was a departure from what most clubs had been—that it marked the start in New York of a trend that was already under way in London, where everyone would converge on a specific night "at a club that was otherwise totally naff." He calls the Savage's predecessors, clubs like Studio 54, Area, the Palladium, "superclubs put together by big investment groups—they wanted to be *the* hot spot in town every night." When Bartsch brought people to the Savage, it was to some place they had never heard of. At Studio 54, with its sod installed around the dance floor for a single night, at Area, with its animals and window displays, at the Palladium, with its wall of video monitors, the decor was part of the show. The Savage was a club completely devoid of decor; the experience consisted of the people and the music. It was, in short, a club that could move around, could convene and adjourn at will. Badum calls it "the born-in-a-wagon-of-a-traveling-show disco event."

When, several months later, Bartsch moved her weekly night to Bentley's, it was because she wanted a club with two dance floors—one for house music, one for disco. It was there, in the beginning of 1988, that she started to bring in strippers, bodybuilders, and drag queens, as go-go dancers. Bartsch says that if she can be credited with some original contribution to nightlife in New York, it's that she took all these people out of their respective corners—the drag queens out of the gay bars, the musclemen out of the gyms, the strippers out of the sex joints—and brought them into her club. With the drag queens, the standard for dressing up was raised even higher. "The nightclub was geared to being able to feature looks," Bartsch says. "I wanted people to come out there and show off their drag. And when I say 'drag' I don't mean that a woman has to turn into a man, or vice versa. I mean, get your goods out of the closet, you know? In England, it's slang for dressing up." By the time Bartsch's bandwagon pulled into the Copacabana, in July of 1988, a good percentage of the customers were turning out in drag as well; the show was no longer confined to the stage.

The setup at the Copa is the same as it was at Bentley's: upstairs, a dark room throbbing to the beat of house music; downstairs, flashing colored lights and disco music. Bartsch says that she encourages people to dress up and "make a statement with themselves." Planning what to wear, shopping, getting ready all put a person in the right frame of mind for having a good time. "I mean, if you don't dress, it's fine with me, too," she says. "It's not, like, a must. But I think it's an important ingredient of energy and successful atmosphere." Marc Jacobs, who has never missed a Copa night, thinks that there's essentially no difference between a drag queen getting dressed to go there and a socialite putting on her haute couture gown for a charity ball; both are going to lengths that designate the evening as special, somehow—that invest it with a certain amount of expectation.

John Badum's guidelines for dressing for Bartsch's events are to break every rule and "go whole hog—and always more makeup." Badum says, "Getting dressed, you think, Oh, God, I feel so ridiculous putting this stuff on all alone at home. But then you get to the club, and everyone else is so over the top that you wish you'd done more."

Nearly everyone, when talking about Bartsch's parties, praises "the energy," describing it as "pure" and "positive," in contrast to the negative or druggy atmosphere of so many other clubs. Ronnie Cooke, a friend of Bartsch's who was for eight and a half years the fashion director of *Details*, says that "Susanne was the first one to make it okay to have fun in New York." Before she ushered in a new era, nightlife here operated according to the same subtle distinctions that regulate life in New York by day: who you are, how much money you make, what you do for a living, who your father was. At clubs like Nell's and, before that, at Studio 54, status was a big part of the package. Club owners then "cast" their clubs the way directors cast a movie, with the audition at the door. Admission was an accomplishment on which the people inside could congratulate themselves; they felt special, chosen, superior to all those poor, shivering hopefuls lined up outside behind the ropes.

The consensus is that Bartsch somehow manages to cross boundaries, to break down the barriers that divide New York into dozens of social ghettos. Uptown types, downtown types, East Siders, West Siders, movie stars, models, businessmen, drag queens—they're all there. One night, she introduced John Badum, who had come as Elizabeth Taylor, to Malcolm Forbes. Marc Jacobs compares Bartsch to party promoters like Nikki Haskell and Carmen d'Alessio, who presided over New York nightlife in the late seventies and early eighties and filled the clubs with Eurotrash. "They were so phony, running around with people with fake titles," he says. "If Susanne is running around with some drag queen with a fake title, it's *deliberately* fake, not trying to be something that it's not." And the deliberate fakery acts as a double negative, proclaiming an authenticity of a different order.

Though Bartsch's nights have for some time now been her main means of support, the money always seems incidental. "You see, I want to do things people can afford, that don't cut a hole in their pockets," she explains. The one exception to her admission policy is the Love Ball, the benefit for the Design Industries Foundation for AIDS that she masterminded in 1989. Moved to action by the news that several friends were sick, Bartsch organized an evening modeled on the house balls popular in Harlem: rigorously stylized send-ups of fashion shows, in which various teams, or "houses," competed in several popular dance forms, including one called vogueing—a sequence of freeze-frame moves based on the highly contrived poses found in old fashion photographs. She persuaded corporations to sponsor the event. People came from all corners of society and paid up to five hundred dollars for their tickets. In the end, the party went down in history as one of the best New York had ever seen and netted over four hundred thousand dollars for the cause. Bartsch calls it "the best thing I've ever done."

This club night Bartsch is now planning in Miami Beach is no charity event, but it has a certain humanitarian agenda, nonetheless. Louis Canales recruited her to help him address what he sees as a serious local problem. When he moved there, in 1986, he found a city so socially segregated that not only, for example, would Cubans refuse to speak to Puerto Ricans, but upper-class Cubans from Coral Gables would have nothing to do with blue-collar Cubans from Hialeah. Canales, who is Cuban-American himself and grew up in New York, has a vision, though he's too modest to call it that: he wants to "build bridges" across these lines and get everybody talking to everybody else. "Not that I'm a knight on a white horse," he says, "but if I'm going to live here I want to make things happen." At first, trusting in the universal language of music and art, he tried producing cultural events and lost a lot of money doing it. "But after being here and going out every night I realized that Miami is a party town," he continues, "and, as pathetic as it may seem, the agora of Miami is going to be the dance floor."

An affable man in his forties who dresses entirely in black, Canales took it upon himself to introduce Bartsch to the owners of a club called Warsaw, on Ocean Drive. For the first party, in November 1990, there was no charge at the door—a gesture that Bartsch considered an investment. For the second, she charged five dollars. This time, she's raising the price to seven to help cover the expenses—plane tickets, taxis, hotel rooms for two deejays and nine drag queens. "I keep them there for three days, so they don't get worn out," she says. "I could send them overnight, but I think that's a bit mean, and I want them to be in good spirits."

On a Thursday evening in January, Bartsch and her husband are installed at 100 Lincoln Road, a crescent-shaped high-rise residence hotel that is set roughly perpendicular to the shore, so that its balconies look straight down the beach. Earlier that afternoon, there had been an altercation at the hotel pool involving Alexis del Lago, a drag queen in her late forties who has come out of retirement in San Juan to work Bartsch's party. To swim in the pool is free; to sit on one of the chaise longues is a dollar. Alexis is indignant that she had to pay to sunbathe, and she explains to Bartsch that, being a diva, she felt justified in pitching a fit. "A diva wouldn't make a fuss about a dollar," Bartsch tells her. "I'll reimburse you." That evening, Bartsch and her husband go out to dinner with Canales, his wife, and Marc Jacobs and his friend Scott Fritz, who have flown in for the party. The conversation turns to drag bars in Tokyo and Paris. In the end, however, everyone agrees that the best drag queens are right here in America. "For sure," Bartsch says. "Better than anywhere." She has been trying to persuade Ty to go to the party tomorrow night in drag. He doesn't seem too keen.

The next day, Bartsch summons the members of her crew to the club at one to help her decorate. But the day is bright, and the warm air has evidently slowed their pace. At one-thirty, a visitor steps into Warsaw's cavernous darkness—black walls, black ceiling, black bar—and finds Susanne cutting crepe-paper streamers, Ty trying to figure out how to work the machine that blows up the balloons, and a handful of stagehand types setting up the lights. Only Mme. Ekathrina Sobechanskaya, otherwise known as Madame, has been by. The founder and director (as Larry Ree) and prima ballerina of the Trockadero Gloxinia Ballet Company, a drag-ballet company based in New York, she stayed long enough to complain about the gels, announced that she was not about to waste her afternoon waiting for "all these queens," and left. One by one, in good time, the others drift in.

Alan Mace, the deejay, who has been with Bartsch since Bentley's, arrives. He says that for these parties in Miami he plays "the latest, most up-to-date New York sound, mostly house music," but that tonight he'll be sharing the booth with Johnny Dynell, another New York deejay, and that they'll mix in some old disco as well. "I don't have a serious attitude about the music," he explains. "I just try to keep the energy up. My emphasis is for everybody to have a good time, so they can drop their worries from the outside world." Mace deejays in drag, as Sister Dimension—affectionately known as Sister. To look up at the booth and see, say, a nurse spinning the records "adds to the madness," he explains.

Gina Germaine shows up wearing high heels, jeans, and a lacy black bra that puckers slightly across the cups, the way a young girl's does when she doesn't quite fill it out. "Cowabunga, dudes," she greets the guys working on the lights. She insists on being identified as "New York's Most Popular Party Girl." "Write it down," she commands, in a breathy contralto. Her show clothes are designed by her dressmaker, Dorian Corey, who lives in Harlem; everything else she buys off the rack. She works all over—in the Poconos, in Richmond, as well as at the Copa. "Mostly, I just walk around and look beautiful and let everybody else dance," she says. She has brought six changes of costume for tonight, and when she's asked to describe the look she has been doing lately she answers, "Suzanne Somers in Las Vegas—healthy, substantial, powerful, aggressive."

Baroness Ostentasia Vulgari—called Baroness for short, with the accent on the "-ess"—travels with a thirty-six-inch Pullman on wheels, a wig case, and a monogrammed Louis Vuitton train case to carry her jewels. She began working Bartsch's parties a year ago, when she turned up at the Copa wearing a look Bartsch liked and was hired. What was the look? "Very high-fashion glamour, yet trashy," she explains. Baroness as a character—and Baroness *is* a character, complete with a European past, a trail of ex-husbands (some dead, some divorced), scandalous rumors that dog her, and an extensive collection of jewels that are her trophies—was born one night when her alter ego, otherwise known as Joseph, decided to go to a club in drag for the first time. "I was with a friend," she explains, "and when we got there I said to him, 'Look at the line outside this club. I'm too old to wait on line—I did that years ago. Let's go home.' He said, 'No, no, no, get out of the cab and see what happens.' I got out of the cab. The doorperson parted the crowd and opened up those velvet ropes. And I have to tell you this: every time those velvet ropes open up for me, it's still a thrill, no matter how many times it happens."

Mathú Andersen, who was born and brought up in Australia and moved to New York in 1988, is a makeup artist and hairdresser for fashion sittings. "I'm a drag queen, but I don't try to look like a woman, because I'm a six-foot man with a man's face," he explains. "So I don't wear fake breasts or do horrendous things to my genitals to get them out of the way. I'm more of a creature, really." Mathú is half of a double act with his friend Zaldy, a delicate young man with exotic Filipino features and silky black hair down to his waist. In drag, they often dress alike. A recent graduate of the Fashion Institute of Technology, Zaldy is, for the time being, happy doing what he calls "custom stuff," like the Lady Miss Kier's costumes for Deee-Lite's next video. Of the designers working today, he admires Thierry Mugler in particular. Mugler knows Bartsch: he's been to the Copa, and many people have suggested that the clothes he's been designing lately follow her example. "Oh, yeah," Zaldy says, "Susanne has definitely inspired him in a big way. His clothes are getting nastier and scantier, and it's really from her parties."

At nine-thirty that evening, Madame comes to the door of her suite in her bathrobe, pours a peach schnapps for me and one for herself, and suggests that her enormous album of press clippings might be of interest while she finishes applying her makeup in the bathroom. Soon she emerges wearing a long Chinese-style sheath, of black velvet and white satin, with black medium-heeled pumps, long white satin gloves, pearl-drop earrings, and a pearl headdress. "Pardon me while I get a fan," she says in a vaguely Russian-accented falsetto. I mention a recent rumor that she is planning to return to the stage. "I have never stopped performing," she replies testily. I ask her about the calendar-girl contest that Bartsch runs here in Miami, as a way of encouraging the local drag queens to turn out. "Ooh," she says, shuddering. "Change the subject on that, darling. That's so *feeble*." I say that I understand she spent the afternoon sewing. "I was hoping that we could talk about something a little more serious," Madame snaps, "but I guess it's not possible."

"Of course it's possible," I reassure her.

"Well," she replies indignantly, "I don't know why I don't get any serious questions."

The doorbell rings. Baroness enters, wearing a strawberry-pink wig and walking friskily in gold lamé spike heels: she has come for help with her dress—a short gold stretch affair with big, square paillettes, the hemline creeping above the tops of her purple stockings, which are hoisted by a garter belt. "*Pardon*," Madame says, in French. "We go in the dressing room."

After Baroness leaves, I ask Madame about the tradition of drag in America. "You know, drag is a very derogatory word in America," she says. "So I always say one shouldn't even mention it." After a moment's consideration, she adds, "I can say I've seen drag for over thirty years in every form, and I think right now it's at the worst it can get. Years ago, when people dragged up, they sat down and designed the dress, went to look for the fabric and the bones and the stays and then for the corset that would work underneath the dress, and they'd have it all made—have the nylons made and have the shoes created and dyed to match the whole. There's no one who does that anymore, ex-

132

cept maybe myself. No one. In my time, all of us did it. All of us. Now they're happy to slap on two little lashes and a pot of rouge and wrap half a yard of fabric around themselves, and then they can sing along with anyone they want to on the records, and good-bye. Bah to them! What is drag? It means so much to so many people. Most people who find it offensive are homophobic. That's another element of it—you have to broach it, whether you want to deal with it or not."

On the way to Warsaw just after midnight, a small posse that includes Jacobs and Fritz runs into Mathú and Zaldy, dressed as twin ostriches and heading back to the hotel for a costume change. A line winds around one side of the club. On the lookout at the door is Ty, wearing a long platinum wig, white platform sandals, a white Playtex-style bra, and a long-line girdle. "That's love," Fritz says.

Inside, Sister Dimension is manning the deejay booth in Martian drag, wearing an Azzedine Alaïa–style acid-green stretch halter body-suit, which clings to the contours of a fake rear end, and huge arched eyelashes, pointy ears, and antennas that bob in time to the music. Baroness has changed wigs: now she's sporting a silver tinsel China chop. Upstairs, Alexis del Lago is holding court in a navy-and-white silk charmeuse sailor top and palazzo pants, with a matching beret. The crowd is disproportionately male and bare-chested. There are, however, plenty of contestants for the Miss January pageant, which is finally won by a queen in a down-market version of local housewife drag, who is wearing a shapeless dress and, as a headpiece, a high tower of bright pink plastic curlers; she is carrying a bag of Doritos and a can of Diet Pepsi. Wandering the dance floor is a cowgirl shooting her pistols; a square-jawed lifeguard type in black-and-white-striped trunks and a jester's cap; a bathing beauty wearing a hot-pink tank suit and a ribbon, bandolier-style, that reads MISS NICARAGUA, and carrying roses; and one lost soul in khaki pants and an argyle vest. Front and center is Bartsch herself, dancing to her heart's content, in a Brazilian Mardi Gras getup—a "cape" of white marabou over a white bra and white draped bikini briefs, and a white sequined skull-cap topped with gigantic white ostrich plumes.

A man sidles up to where I'm standing on the sidelines and offers to buy me a drink. I ask if he's come to Bartsch's nights before. This is the first time, he replies, but he's been to Warsaw on two other occasions—always at the insistence of his roommate, he hastily explains, who is gay. A silence falls between us as our attention settles on a completely bald man, familiar as a model for Robert Mapplethorpe's photographs, wearing a crinoline and dancing on top of a nearby go-go box. "Sad, isn't it?" the bystander says.

"What's sad?" I ask.

"All these misfits wishing they were something they're not. There are a lot of tragic people in this room." Well, I thought to myself, they certainly don't *look* sad. I remembered something that Jacobs had said that afternoon: that Bartsch's parties always make him think of kids who weren't accepted by their peers, because they were too effeminate, or too short, or too wide, or too whatever. And now all those outcasts have come together in this disco *salon des refusés* that Bartsch is running, and together they have found their revenge. While their persecutors have grown up to live life by the book, upholding the conventions by which they are deemed attractive or important or successful, the so-called freaks are reveling in their freakishness and having such great fun doing it that they've turned the tables. Now it's the so-called normal people who are the outsiders, looking in.

On a snowy weekday afternoon in mid-December, in Manhattan, when holiday shoppers are thronging the aisles of Saks Fifth Avenue, when parents and their children line up behind velvet ropes to file past the storybook windows at Lord & Taylor, the traffic is, quite frankly, rather light at Lee's Mardi Gras, purveyor of women's clothes and accessories, underwear, and makeup—for men. One of the store's managers, who goes by the name of "Bubbles," attributes this to Lee's no-returns, no-exchanges policy, which was initiated to discourage fetishists from using an item once and bringing it back. All sales at Lee's, you may rest assured, are final. For those who are not entirely confident of their skill in selecting the perfect present, Lee's offers gift certificates. Even so, the store is in no danger of being overrun by the midtown crowds, for any number of reasons. For one, there is no sign, nothing visible from the street—the westernmost block of Fourteenth Street, in the city's meat-packing district—to direct the prospective customer to the third-floor loft that is Lee's.

The metal door downstairs opens directly into the building's elevator, which on this particular afternoon has been commandeered by the cast and crew of a kung-fu movie being shot in the loft on five. From time to time, a customer squeezes in among the coffee urns and sound equipment and boxes of catered sandwiches being ferried up-stairs from the street and emerges finally, triggering the bell at the store's entrance. Then Lee or Terry or whoever is minding the office comes out to stand behind the white Formica counter. "Hello," he says, in a tone that is cordial and welcoming but not chummy or in-quisitive. In the spirit of the season, the store is festooned with tinsel garlands draped around the walls and cut-out snowflakes hanging from the fluorescent lights. The radio is tuned to Z-100, a local top-forty station.

Many of Lee's customers make a beeline for the shoe department, in the rear, with its potted palm in the corner, its armless chrome-and-vinyl chairs like the ones in hotel dining rooms, its new carpet—a six-by-nine area rug, banded white, which Lee claims smells like a skunk—covering the linoleum floor. "Every rug I saw had fringe on it," he says, by way of explaining why he chose this particular one, "and I hate fringe."

"Since when?" Dixie, a veteran drag queen and a longtime cus-tomer, retorts.

The shoes are ranged on shelves, mounted on pegboard walls, or displayed on freestanding racks that revolve at a languid pace. There are faux-crocodile pumps and slingback sandals and patent-leather T-straps and marabou-trimmed satin mules and Mary Janes like the ones schoolgirls wear, all of them enormous-looking. As women's shoes go, these have a little more glitz (lace trim, rhinestones, lamé) than most, and also more straps, the better to fasten them to feet un-accustomed to walking in something so precarious and fragile. Lee tells a customer, a towering man trying on pumps with four-inch heels, what every woman knows from experience: "As the shoe stretches, which it will, you'll slide more into the toe."

Two black women—one of them, upon closer inspection, a man—are admiring a black mule banded with gold braid at the instep. "I wish I could wear heels," the one in drag says. "These are funky." She is wearing boots with flat crepe soles. She lingers in front of the spike-heeled, thigh-high red vinyl boots. "I guess I'll get a bra and panty to match," she tells her friend. "I'm looking for something that Eric will like. He wanted me to get a red negligee."

The lingerie is arranged in bin drawers, according to style and size. The variety is staggering: underwire bras, soft-cup bras, stretch bras, push-up bras, bikini bras, padded bras, even padded-shoulder bras (with the pads built out from the straps); in lace, in polyester charmeuse, in silver lamé, in leopard-spotted crepe, in red satin strewn with white hearts, in black rubber studded with nailheads; in colors like red, pink, ivory, and "champagne." Lee stocks what he has been told (by Broadway costume designers looking to clothe a long line of flat-chested chorus girls) is the city's largest selection of bras in size 32A. (The store also carries a remarkable array of false eyelashes, feather boas, and fishnet tights.) For every bra Lee's sells, there's a matching brief or thong or tap pant or G-string. There are also bustiers, waist cinchers, and padded long-line girdles, for molding the recalcitrant male form; teddies, garter belts, and Merry Widows, for lounging at home the way the models do in the Victoria's Secret catalogue; panty girdles, "gartinis" (panties with garters attached), "pettislips," and other paraphernalia which, despite the fact that it is now virtually extinct in most women's wardrobes, is lovingly perpetuated here as an integral part of the standard-issue femininity kit.

Lee's Mardi Gras has been in business for twenty-four years now, the past five of them in this location, with mail-order customers all over the world. In New York, Bubbles says, the store's only significant competition is Patricia Field, but she caters to the customers he calls the "bar queens," who are, in comparison with the average Lee's customer, "way-out." Also, he adds, she doesn't have nearly the selection that Lee's does. According to Bubbles, Halloween is the busiest day of the year, every year, with people shopping for complete outfits at five P.M. As for the catalogue items, these days Lee's is having a hard time keeping up with the demand. Some of the shoes have been on back-order for seven weeks, and not long ago it took five and a half months to get a new shipment of push-up bras.

Lee subscribes to *Women's Wear Daily*, to keep up with fashion trends and with what's happening in the large-size women's market. But the considerable progress that has lately been made for women who are size fourteen and up hasn't been such a boon for the men who are Lee's constituency—not only because women's large sizes tend to be cut short-waisted and big in the hips, which is all wrong for a man, but also because most "full-figured" women would never wear the very styles that Lee's customers crave, for fear of looking even bigger and more conspicuous. There is, Bubbles laments, a terrible dearth of fringed dresses in sizes 20 and 22. Lee and his staff are always on the lookout for new sources, but by now, Bubbles says, the store is so well established that most manufacturers come to them. Like any good boutique with clients who get invited to all the same parties, Lee's buys only one or two of a dress in each size, "so that people don't see themselves coming and going," Bubbles explains.

The labels read like slightly scrambled designer names: "Arman Originals," "Argenti," "Andrea Kristoff for Escante." There are lots of knits, beloved for their capacity to adapt to bodies whose proportions don't conform to the garment industry's size charts. There are also, surprisingly, a good many suits and two-piece dresses, for daytime—for the man who lives drag. At first glance, the clothes Lee's has to offer are not much different from those that fill the racks of most large-size women's departments, proving, perhaps, that the goals of women who wear large sizes and of men who wear women's clothes are more or less the same: to camouflage what fashion magazines used to call their "figure flaws," to look smaller all over. But a closer look at Lee's inventory reveals a little more flamboyance—brighter colors and more lamé and beads and sequins—than most large-size women go in for. These are clothes for big women with big personalities, not the kind who are looking to blend into the background. Even so, the prevailing style is, oddly, rather matronly—more along the lines of the mother of the bride than of the bride herself, let alone of the femme fatale who stops men dead in their tracks.

A dress in purple changeable taffeta, deep blue in the folds, has been engineered to cover up those areas that are an overweight woman's trouble spots—areas that, as it happens, can be dead giveaways on a man: short ruffled sleeves to conceal the upper arms and shoulders, a drop waistline to disguise the lack of any indentation, a draped bodice and a gathered skirt to make for a more graceful illusion; a dainty taffeta rose has been affixed to one hip. The most expensive dress at Lee's is a six-hundred-dollar evening gown, a black sheath beaded and sequined in a floral pattern. A man who works in the fashion business and does drag on a regular basis, who buys his shoes at Lee's, turns up his nose at the clothes. "Ugh, so suburban," he says. "This is for mall queens."

The bell at the elevator rings and a customer appears: a man with salt-and-pepper hair and a mustache. He is wearing a navy Chesterfield coat over a dark suit that seems more Madison Avenue than Wall Street. "Just looking," he replies when Terry asks if there's anything he can help him with. Eventually, he disappears into the fitting room with a black-and-white polka-dot organza dress.

The fitting room at Lee's is off to the right, by the wigs and the makeup and the extra-tall panty hose. One wall is exposed brick, painted white. There's a folding wooden curtain, for privacy, and a big cylindrical water heater in the corner. The walls are decorated with posters, imaginary portraits of famous men in drag: Sylvester Stallone as a blonde, in denim cutoffs; Idi Amin, wearing slacks and a sweater; Robert Redford, with a Dolly Parton hairdo; Jimmy Carter; Charles Bronson; Johnny Cash.

Between customers, Bubbles and Terry and Dixie sit on the chairs in the shoe department and shoot the breeze, like residents of a small town, congregating at the general store. Every so often, Lee takes a break from the paperwork in the office and comes out and joins them. In a voice thick with an accent from his native Mississippi, Dixie tells the story of the pearl earrings he saved his allowance to buy when he was ten; he gave them to his mother. Every time she left him alone in the house, he says, he would put them on, along with her fur pieces— stone martens, in a town where all the other ladies had run-of-the-mill minks—and parade around the house, then hastily put everything back in its place before she got home. One day, however, his mother got back and something sparkling on the rug in the living room caught her eye. She picked it up: it was an eye from one of the stone martens. "She beat my ass to a salad," Dixie says. After her aunt died and left her good earrings, his mother never wore costume jewelry again, and not long ago Dixie asked her for the pearl earrings. He wore them to a dance. "It took forty years," he says triumphantly, "but I got 'em on."

Terry entertains the assembled with tales of his days working at a strip joint in Chicago, where the management booked drag acts to alternate with the strippers, to make the entertainment a little classier.

On this particular afternoon Terry is dressed in a sweatshirt and jeans, sneakers, and a New York Yankees baseball cap, with two gold hoops in his left ear, one in his right, and a red-rhinestone-studded AIDS-awareness ribbon brooch. It is difficult to picture him in a dress, if only because his body seems wide in all the wrong places. This particular strip joint, he continues, made its money on the drinks, which—highballs and martinis and Manhattans alike—came in shallow plastic champagne glasses with ice, so as to leave the least possible room for liquid. The management had a policy for encouraging employees to cajole the customers into buying them drinks: Terry would ask for a screwdriver, which cost six dollars and, inevitably, arrived without the vodka. He saved the plastic stirrer until the end of the week, when he and the other drag performers and the strippers would cash in their stirrers for a dollar apiece. The strippers, Terry recalls, were so afraid of theft in the dressing rooms that they would carry their handbags full of plastic stirrers onstage with them, when they did their acts.

The bell rings again, and a Japanese businessman comes in. Bubbles offers to be of some assistance. The man is here from Tokyo, where he has heard about Lee's, he explains in piecemeal English. He would like to see what there is. "Be my guest," Bubbles tells him, at which he seems confused. Bubbles leaves him free to browse. Ten minutes later, after a quick tour of the rest of the store, the man is in the makeup department, studiously examining the Max Factor Overnight Moisture Supplement, the fluorescent hair spray, the Strong Hold Nail Wrap Kit, the body and leg makeup, the powder puffs, the eyelash adhesive, the wigs with names like Madonna, Mona Lisa, Brigitte, Vogue, and Cosmo. He picks up the gift-boxed set of Le Jardin d'Amour perfumed bath powder and eau de toilette spray, and turns it over in his hands. He scrutinizes the displays for Incognito, "The Romantic Fragrance, from Cover Girl" ("The intrigue never ends . . .") and for Clarion lipsticks: "How To Wear Red! Red. Right, and perfect on you. A crimson signature. A complete look. Matched. Marvelous. A girl's gotta have it." Finally, his attention comes to rest on a poster, a composite of George Hurrell–style portraits of Hollywood's leading ladies. "The name behind the most glamorous faces for over 75 years," it announces. "Max Factor. The Glamour goes on."

Holly came from Miami, F-L-A,
Hitchhiked her way across the U.S.A.
Plucked her eyebrows on the way,
Shaved her legs and then he was a she,
She said, "Hey, babe, take a walk on the wild side."

Lou Reed,
"Walk on the Wild Side"

Hugh Steers is the first to admit that his style of painting isn't fashionable in the New York art world of the nineties. He says this without rancor, as a statement of fact. Despite favorable reviews and a loyal, if not large, following, his work isn't much in keeping with the stuff that lines the walls at Mary Boone, or Metro Pictures, or any of the other galleries that are the unofficial headquarters for what's happening. It's not the subject matter that's the problem—Steers is only one of many artists dealing with AIDS and homosexuality and transvestism, and many of them are more successful than he is. It's the fact that he plays out these themes in figurative paintings without irony, as if he were serious about speaking a language coined by Michelangelo, Titian, Rubens, Delacroix, and Manet, among others—a language loaded with the heavy weight of history.

In *White Satin*, one butch-looking man in a tank top that shows off his bulging biceps helps another man, who is wearing a black mini-dress and high heels, into a white satin coat. A double bed is seen in the background; the floor is a checkerboard of black-and-white linoleum—like the floors that delineate the space of the rooms in Vermeer's paintings.

In *Denim Jacket*, a man lies on his side, his back to the viewer, naked, looking over his shoulder at a woman standing beside the bed, getting dressed to leave. The eponymous jacket, hung over the back of a chair, could belong to either of them. The wall is yellow; the floor, black-and-white tiles in a chicken-wire pattern.

In *Two Men and a Woman*, an emaciated man, his eyes half-closed in dull pain or semiconscious exhaustion, is seen from above lying in a tub, attended by a woman and a man—his parents, perhaps—who bathe him. The floor is a grid of white ceramic tiles.

These and other scenes are rendered in the light-filled, lyrical style that Pierre Bonnard reserved for the body of his mistress set in some cozy interior. The disparity between the paintings' lush surface and the events they depict is startling and intentional. The Impressionist overtones—evoking a period beloved of art collectors and corporations—seduce the viewer into a world of gender dysphoria and fatal disease, but Steers insists that this is not a ploy. "If you want people to get involved and think about these difficult subjects," he says, "then you have to give them something in return." What he offers is a sensuous presentation, the sheer beauty of the brush strokes on the canvas, which in the end serves to dignify these themes that are more often, and more predictably, portrayed in sordid tones. The result, he hopes, will be suffused with the same sort of "gorgeous bleakness" that to Steers's mind is one of the distinguishing characteristics of great American art—in works by painters as diverse as Edward Hopper and Franz Klein and Jackson Pollock.

"Too open" is the standard premise for rejection of Steers's work by the big galleries, most of which would prefer a little less emotion up front. Steers says he feels like he's constantly walking "the knife edge of sentimentality" in his paintings, the danger being that at any moment they could dissolve into bathos, but he's willing to run this risk for the sake of an outcome that is in some way "more humanist" than the safe distance that comes with, say, a more conceptual approach. The voyeurism that runs throughout his work has not gone unremarked. Critics have written about the paintings' closed-off quality— a tight, perspectival space, delineated in many cases by the formal pattern of the floors and inhabited by people who never make eye contact with the viewer, whose backs are often turned. The only exchange is among the characters, with the painting's surface like a fourth wall, however transparent; there is no way in. The viewer experiences what Steers calls the "exquisite embarrassment" of witnessing some intimate moment.

Steers's work is notable for its refusal to sensationalize material that is by definition potentially sensational. Drag queens in his paintings are never camp: they wear no wigs or makeup, only women's clothes that are, to his way of thinking, an expression of some aspect of their personality. "The vulnerability implicit in high heels or a tight skirt is part of their nature," he explains. Steers says that his repeated choice of drag queens as a subject has to do, at least in part, with their marginal status in society. He compares them to artists, to homosexuals, to harlequins (a man in a painting called *Harlequin Slip* wears a diamond-patterned slip that invokes Picasso's clowns)—all of whom play out their lives beyond convention, on the outskirts of power.

Steers says that he has never dressed in drag himself, notwithstanding the sober black ankle-length skirt he wore—with men's shoes—to his senior dinner at Yale. The effect was elegant and understated, he claims, befitting his WASP background (summers in Newport, boarding school in Connecticut). Even so, he is fascinated by clothes and their capacity to enhance certain erotic aspects not only of the female body—their usual function—but of the male body as well. High heels, for instance, "set off the shape of the calf," he explains. "They make a man's leg look great, too."

Transvestism relies heavily on symbols, a vocabulary that Steers believes is not confined to clothes. A high-heeled shoe is a symbol of femininity, but so are certain gestures, he contends. In the painting in which the woman is leaving the man in bed, Steers took great pleasure in reversing the roles and assigning her one of the classic male gestures: she is zipping her fly. The drag queen not only puts on a woman's white satin coat, she does it with a woman's gesture: the passive shrug she can afford only when someone is standing behind her, guiding her arms into the sleeves.

Steers figures that the trappings of femininity are just as hard for some women to put on as they are for most football players, and he believes that those women shouldn't be forced into clothes that misrepresent them. "But then," he says, "there are men out there who run around in six-inch spike-heeled platforms like they're wearing high-top sneakers—they love it, and I think that's great." Born in 1962, in Bethesda, Maryland, Steers belongs to a generation raised, in America, in the midst of widespread confusion over sex roles. Like many people, he has spent a lot of time trying to make sense of the standard definitions as they apply to his own experience. He frequently discussed these things with his mother, a writer; his wrists, he says, are smaller than hers.

Steers has come to the conclusion that the whole spectrum—from hyper-masculinity to hyper-femininity, and including everything in between—should be available to people of both sexes all the time, that the world would be a better place if society embraced all the possibilities. The androgyny that was the hope of the seventies, a demilitarized zone where men and women could meet and adopt the best traits of both sexes, strikes Steers as a unlikely solution. It would be nice, he allows, if everyone were taken on his or her own terms, as a person, without being sized up as a man or as a woman. But the inconvenient fact of the matter is that these things are not so easy to legislate when it comes to sex. And sex in all its particulars, Steers says—"the things that feel good and rock your world"—is so often "so politically incorrect."

....

For a brief moment back in the early nineties, mega-stardom seemed just around the corner: that was when *Paris Is Burning*, Jennie Livingston's award-winning documentary about the Harlem drag balls, won an Oscar, not long after Madonna seized on the dance style that grew out of those balls, with her hit single, "Vogue." In Livingston's film, the drag queens confided to the camera with heartbreaking candor about all the things they wanted—a washing machine, a refrigerator—as if the camera itself might make those things possible at last. Meanwhile, there was Willy Ninja, champion voguer—a cross between Olga Korbut and Dovima—working it front and center in Madonna's video, in heavy rotation on MTV. Suddenly, the future, which had been narrow, if not closed, for drag queens and ball children, looked to be wide open.

Ninja's career has since stalled; Dorian Corey, Crystal LaBeija, Kim Pendavis, Angie Xtravaganzo—the living "legends" of the ball houses—have died, victims of murder or a heart attack or AIDS. The "crossover appeal" has waned. Though the ball houses continued, most degenerated into gangs whose primary concern was not "walking" categories their founders had made famous but shoplifting and kiting checks.

Even so, the balls continued, too, retreating for a few years to the Midwest, returning to New York without a lot of fanfare. By 1997, the TV crews are gone. The days of SRO crowds at the Harlem Elks Club and a seemingly endless roster of some forty categories, lasting well past dawn, are over, at least for the time being. In their place, a miniseries of "mini-balls" has sprung up, with fewer categories and a more no-nonsense approach to the proceedings.

Picture a bowling alley: not a real one, with pins and gutters, but a room roughly the size and shape of three lanes. At the far end is a tiny stage, two steps up, where the judges preside. Along the walls on either side, two rows of chairs are lined up behind police barricades; between them lies the runway. This is Planet 28, a small club on a street that gentrification has overlooked, in the shadow of the Fashion Institute of Technology's dormitory.

Billed as a "Mini-Night of Legends, Statements & Stars, Part II," the goings-on one Wednesday in July, postmidnight, are a rapid-fire, abbreviated version of the programs that used to unfold at a leisurely pace. Even the drag is in shorthand—none of that head-to-toe, over-the-top, simulated glam; a simple handbag says it all, provided you hold it correctly. The categories have been reduced to a mere twelve: seven in the Butch Queen division, including "Sandal Scandal 1997 w/Eyewear," and five in the Femme Queen division.

Kevin Ultra Omni, the "mother" of the House of Ultra Omni, who is also one of the evening's organizers and, intermittently, its emcee, has gathered a handful of "legends" to serve as judges. Larry Ebony, original "father" of the House of Ebony, who moved to Texas, is back this evening. Marcel Christian, one of the stars of *Paris Is Burning*, is here, in a red jersey off-the-shoulder tunic and pants that look like something Helmut Lang might have designed for *Flashdance*. Richard Ebony, "son" of Larry, past winner in such categories as "Hi Fashion Evening Wear, Leather v. Suede" and "Wilhelmina Face," takes his place behind the table set up on the dais; he is also a schoolteacher, Ultra Omni notes with pride—"not just a trophy winner but an educator." Many of the city's leading houses—among them, Chanel, Moschino, Bazaar, Mugler, Prada, Mizrahi, Armani—have turned out to compete. "This doesn't have to be nine thousand people," Ultra Omni announces over a P.A. system that fills in the spaces between his words with static. "But if it's the right people, it's ovah!" ("Ovah" is an expression of excellence, not to be confused with "over".)

A solidly built black man who looks to be in his late thirties, Kevin Ultra Omni is wearing a latex stocking cap stretched tight over his skull, clear plastic goggles, a plaid shirt, and baggy shorts that stop below the knees. He introduces some of his "children" who have turned out tonight: the legendary Brian ("not only a face but also an artist—he had his paintings up at Thirty-six Federal Plaza"), Tanya ("the psychiatrist of the house—she works in a hospital, she takes care of crazy people"), and Pleasure Ultra Omni ("a professional model—just give me one model walk, Pleasure, start with the pose"). "I love all my kids," he says, in summation. "They're not all here tonight. We been together seventeen years."

Ultra Omni is out to educate a new generation of ball "children," most of them unaware of the tradition's distinguished history. Like many children, these are incapable of sitting still and listening for very long. They talk among themselves; he talks over them, telling them a little something about his own background. "My first trophy I ever won was Butch Queen First Time in Drag," he says, warming to his subject. "And I felt very good because I never did it before, never practiced in my mother's kitchen, and I won the grand prize. And I was scared, wearing those pumps. And believe me, there was plenty of competition.

"After that, I walked the category called Best Dressed Man, and won grand prize.

"Then I came for realness, and won grand prize.

"My last award was at the Latex Ball—that was my one-hundredth trophy award. Others did it in reverse order, but I did it the hard way: first, I told you I was a woman; then I told you I was a man; then I told you I was real."

Sharing the stage is Kevin Aviance, club diva and sometime deejay, whose rhythm track with a vamp serves as the background for Selvin Mizrahi's rap—the *legendary* Selvin Mizrahi from the *legendary* House of Mizrahi.

Ultra Omni announces the first category: "Butch Queen Realness," to be followed by "Butch Realness, Uptown v. Downtown." "You should not have to decide if you're real or not," he advises the contestants. "Anybody walking?" Mizrahi asks, keeping the beat. Larry Ebony walks. "Anybody else dare to come behind the legendary Larry Ebony?" No takers. "Yes, no, maybe, so let me know on the count of three," Mizrahi keeps up the patter. For "Butch Realness," Ultra Omni defines "butch" as either a man or "a male impersonator" (which could also be a man). "You fucking bitches, follow the beat," Mizrahi scolds, still rapping. "Bring it, work it, serve it."

The chief difference between competitors in the butch and femme categories would seem to be attitude, not wardrobe. The clothes, with Polo, Nautica, and Tommy Hilfiger logos prominently displayed, are surprisingly unisex, though the women—biological and otherwise— seem more inclined to something tight, like a tank top. The closest to full-out drag this evening ever gets comes in a category called "Mary Got a Bad Perm & She's Late for the Omni Ball," won by one J. J. Aphrodite, wearing a roller in her hair, a housecoat, glasses, and a Birkenstock on one foot, a Manolo Blahnik spike-heeled sandal held on with packing tape on the other.

Next category: "Team Runway," requiring "1 Butch Queen Vogue Femme and 1 Femme Queen Vogue Dramatical Cunt." Five teams take the floor, squaring off in pairs, each dancing a three-minute round to Aviance's song "Cunty." Eric Bazaar takes over as emcee, shouting encouragement: "Fierce back! Fierce with love!" In the end, it comes down to a duel between an anonymous Asian contestant and Albert Revlon, both of them manic and determined. "Suzy Wong! Anna Sui! Madame Butterfly! Beans and rice!" Bazaar cheers on the Asian, whose inventory of poses seems endless, with no more than a split second between them. In reply, Revlon body-slams the floor, contorts his arms and legs into shapes a pretzel couldn't get into. This is mortal combat; the final match at Wimbledon looks like friendly Ping-Pong by comparison. And the decision of the judges is: Revlon, who steps up to the stage to collect his reward, a cheap trophy invested with the hopes of his competitors, and runs, screaming, through the crowd and out into the night.

ASYMMETRY

In presenting the habits and behaviour of a man, she was still very much a woman. She was presenting a woman's idea of a man, or rather, her attitude to a certain kind of male behaviour to which she was often subjected.

Samuel Pepys,

in his diary, on a performance by Nell Gwynn

....

The flyer for Diane Torr's Drag Kings Workshop—an all-day course for women looking to dress up as men—promises assistance in the creation of a masculine guise and instruction in masculine body language and conduct. "Just learning the behavior is useful in career advancement," the notice continues, "or even in something as simple as getting your full share of a seat on the subway!"

Not long after I had signed up for the workshop, I was on the phone with a friend, a man whose manner is routinely described as "flamboyant." I told him about the workshop's methods and goals.

"Darling!" he exclaimed. "Take me with you!"

"I can't," I replied. "The flyer says 'for women only.'"

"That's not fair!" he sulked. "I want to learn how to be a man!"

The course was not to be entered into lightly. "Please think very carefully about the kind of man you would like to become," the flyer had urged, "and bring the appropriate outfit." Nor, I decided, was it to be entered into alone. Another friend, an art dealer, had agreed to come along. "What kind of guy do I want to be?" the art dealer wondered aloud, a week in advance. "The kind of guy I like or the kind of guy I hate?" Being several sizes smaller than her husband, she balked at the prospect of having to buy a suit.

"You don't have to wear a suit," I assured her.

"I do if I'm going to be a CEO," she insisted.

I confessed that I approached the workshop with some trepidation. "Suppose I look in the mirror and realize that I'm much better looking as a man than as a woman?" I ask.

My friend laughed. "That's ridiculous," she said.

Drag is—to state the obvious—not symmetrical. The bars in Bangkok are filled with men dressed as women; there are no women dressed as men. Carnaval, in Rio, which grants men the right to appear in public in the clothes of the opposite sex, would presumably grant the same right to women, if only they would take it. On the ferry that serves as troop carrier for the Fourth of July invasion of the Pines, on Fire Island, the guys turned out as Marilyn Monroe or Liza Minnelli or Linda Evangelista by far outnumber the women dressed as Indian chiefs or baseball players.

The tradition of women in drag is admittedly slender but long and not undistinguished. Historians have documented cases as far back as the end of the sixteenth century. Up until the start of World War II, women dressed as men primarily to arrogate the small, everyday freedoms that men claimed as their birthright. But if drag was a means to an end, the end was more benign in some cases than in others. There are picaresque tales of one woman who, out of patriotism, became a soldier and was subsequently decorated for her bravery, and of another who became a buccaneer. A lovestruck woman went to war in drag alongside her husband so as not to be separated from him; a disgruntled wife dressed in drag in order to keep her adultery a secret. We learn of the lone female traveler who adopted men's clothes as a safety precaution, and of the thief whose getaway was facilitated by her disguise. Here was a bride-to-be desperate to evade her repugnant betrothed; there, a fortune hunter who, masquerading as a man, courted the daughter of a wealthy merchant for the sake of her sizable dowry.

It was only toward the end of the eighteenth century that female transvestism came to be linked with a lesbian sexual preference. In fact, the evidence suggests that men could find a woman in drag alluring, provided that she somehow let it be known that she was a woman. Odd as this notion may seem, and despite the enormous changes in women's lives and dress that have transpired since, the sex appeal of a woman in drag survives: we can sense it, in our time, in the slightly sinister thrill that lurks just beneath the surface in Helmut Newton's photographs of women wearing tuxedos. It is a thrill that the sight of a man in drag rarely, if ever, induces in a woman.

As for drag's capacity to unsettle the viewer, it could be argued that the more complete the transformation in a man's case, the less threatening it is. The man who closely approximates a woman challenges our thinking only when we finally realize that she is a man, and even then the chances are that we will find her not offensive or off-putting but disarming. By demonstrating that a man can "become" a woman, he confirms the message our culture sends via advertisements, magazines, movies: that femininity is predicated on artifice and therefore can be acquired. Being a woman—or being the kind of woman considered attractive and desirable—requires an effort. (RuPaul, the New York drag queen, made a brief, unsuccessful bid for pop stardom with a song called "You'd Better Work.") It's the drag queen who attempts and fails (or refuses) to conceal her identity as a man who is far more likely to make us uncomfortable, by confronting us with an image of compromised masculinity.

When it comes to women in drag, however, the situation is reversed: it's the partial transformation—the "butch" woman—that's easier to take in stride, while the woman who seems completely plausible as a man calls into question our standards of masculinity. Unlike femininity, which relies on makeup, on clothes that contort and exaggerate the shape of the body, masculinity has been construed as "natural," inimitable, indomitable—strictly the province of men. If a woman can convincingly simulate a man, then there must be something wrong with masculinity: it has failed to hold its ground; it has been proven impotent in the face of a woman's raid on its demeanor and appearance. While a man in drag may in fact uphold the ideology of femininity, a woman in drag is liable to undermine the ideology of masculinity.

Paradoxically, and apart from whatever threats they may have posed, women who have worn men's clothes have historically been regarded as noble souls, aspiring to some higher order of being. The lore of the Catholic church included several saints who, in the course of becoming holy, transcended their femininity and took on the traits of men: Saint Thecla, who abandoned her fiancé and, dressed as a man, joined the retinue of Paul the Apostle; Saint Margaret, who disguised herself in men's clothes to escape her wedding night and subsequently became a monk; Saint Uncumber, a Portuguese princess who prayed to be delivered from her engagement to the heathen King of Sicily and, praise God, grew a beard; to say nothing of Joan of Arc—a more recent addition to the tradition.

The changes in women's lives that have come about over the course of the twentieth century have pretty much rendered obsolete the old incentives to dress in drag. In America, in Europe, in many other parts of the world, women can get an education and a job; they can travel alone, without the armor that a man's suit once provided; they can go to war or go to sea. For that matter, the impact of a woman dressed in drag now is nowhere near what it once was, in the days when pants and short hair were taboo. From where men stand, femininity—with all its accoutrements—is still a long way off, at a safe distance and then some, with a great divide separating them and it. But masculinity, or, at any rate, the access to its trappings, is for most women within hailing distance; women are already halfway there.

If in our time the sight of a woman wearing a mustache and a man's suit is not as resonant as the sight of a man in a dress, if women in drag are somehow lacking in the zeal that animates their male counterparts, perhaps it's for lack of a mission. When they dress as Marilyn Monroe or Brigitte Bardot, drag queens take it upon themselves to perpetuate certain female types, many of which—among women, at least—have died a natural death. Seen in the aftermath of the feminist revolt, male drag can be interpreted as an act of mourning for a variety of womankind soon to be extinct. Women, however, appear to have no such nostalgia for the time-honored male stereotypes: the Cowboy, say, or the Army General or the Football Hero. Many, if not most, women, in fact, would just as soon see these monolithic roles abolished, to make way for a new masculinity, one that is subtler and more nuanced.

And yet, in the face of mass confusion on the part of men and women alike about what exactly a man is supposed to be these days, the types persist. Even the twelve women in Diane Torr's Drag Kings Workshop had a hard time coming up with a new version of a man that didn't seem like a hollow replica of the old kind. A woman who goes out on a blind date asks herself at the end of the evening if she liked the guy enough to see him a second time; the women who, under Torr's direction, became drag kings for a night asked themselves whether they liked the men they had become enough to *be* them a second time, and the answer in the majority of cases was no more auspicious than it usually is after a stilted meeting with an uncongenial stranger.

....

As women, we were a motley group. We arrived on an Indian summer Saturday afternoon at a high-rise apartment building on lower Lexington Avenue, carrying garment bags and satchels containing the sort of outfits that the men we had invented for ourselves would wear, in addition to a few supplies specified on the flyer: "Bring: hair gel, wide bandage to bind breasts (if needed), and fake penis (the most convincing is a piece of tubular bandage, stuffed with cotton wool and sewn at either end—don't make it too large!!)." The doorman nodded wearily when we arrived and went back to the sports section of the *Post*.

A former topless dancer, now a performance artist who works almost exclusively in drag, Diane Torr seems in some respects uniquely qualified to guide a group of women through the metamorphosis from femininity to masculinity. A redhead, wearing black-velvet leggings, a white shirt with a black-velvet collar, and drop earrings, she greeted her new pupils with a hostess's magnanimous welcome (the apartment that served as Torr's classroom on this occasion was borrowed from a friend). As the afternoon wore on into the evening and she changed into men's clothes, she supervised the proceedings with a headmaster's quiet authority.

When, in 1994, Torr offered a class at the New School for Social Research, in New York, the course definition called cross-dressing in performance art "the adopted mode of the avant-garde, . . . opposing and transgressing socially defined codes of behavior. In these times," the catalogue went on to suggest, "it might also be interpreted as a

way to move beyond traditional paradigms of masculine and feminine, binary opposites, established stereotypes, and confining definitions of identity." The curriculum for this particular day, however,
had been billed as somewhat less theoretical and more practical.

As it turned out, this graduating class in Torr's academy comprised
students who hailed from a rather narrow range of professions. Theater, dance, and art were distinctly overrepresented. One woman
worked in the marketing department of a book-publishing house; another was an English major at a local university. We ranged in age
from late teens to mid-forties, and in motives from personal curiosity
to professional ambition.

A reporter named Paula, from *The Washington Post*, recruited five
other women to pose with her for the "before" picture that would ac-
company her story: Peggy and her friend, also named Paula, both
dark-eyed and short-haired, similarly dressed in jeans and black tank
tops; Caroline, another brunette, in jeans and a V-neck T-shirt, her
long hair falling around her shoulders; Char, a sweet-faced blonde, in
a red T-shirt, black leggings, and white cowboy boots; and Diane Torr
herself. They lined up in front of the fish tank, their arms around each
other's waists, shifting uneasily from foot to foot as the photographer
consulted his light meter. "How should we look?" they wondered
aloud. "Just look like women!" Diane replied. This part they knew.

At a table by the door, presiding over an array of fake mustaches,
beards, and sideburns, sat Johnny (also a woman), a special-effects
makeup artist for films: "My expertise is primarily in horror and gore.
I really have no experience in glamour makeup." One by one, the candidates for manhood presented themselves. "Did you have anything
in particular in mind in the way of facial hair?" Johnny asked Maureen, a video artist and sculptor.

One of two friends who had come together had made the other a
penis. "Who didn't bring a penis?" Diane asked. "I have some extra
ones." She offered a selection, arranging them on the kitchen counter.

"You're going to make a very handsome man," Johnny told me,
to my anxiety and dismay. "You have a face that's real matinee-idol
material—you know, the Ronald Colman type."

"Say good-bye to your breasts!" one woman told another as she
wound gaffer's tape around her chest.

Johnny turned his attention to Marianne, the art dealer, applying glue to her upper lip. In the end, she had settled on becoming the kind of guy she rarely, if ever, meets—an insurance salesman living in a Long Island suburb, a drab character in an ill-fitting suit and a light blue, permanent-press, barrel-cuff shirt, which she'd found for three dollars at the Salvation Army.

"Actually," Johnny said, "I'm always amazed—everybody looks so good as a man. Guys, when they dress like women, tend to become homely women. But women, even average-looking women, tend to make handsome guys. The parameters for men are so much broader. There's a lot more leeway."

Waiting our turn for makeup, the women discussed our reasons for enrolling in Torr's course. "My work is very involved in gender issues," Maureen said. "I'm interested in clothing, in the transformations one can go through. Once, as part of a class project, I dressed up as if I were pregnant and went to the Museum of Modern Art. It was an incredible experience, to be somebody other than who I was. There was a whole set of questions people would ask me. 'Did you feel the baby move yet?' Things like that."

Marianne called the workshop "a chance to get out of yourself and see the world through a different lens."

Caroline, a self-described "nonprofit hag"—a media artist who also teaches, and works as a film and video curator—had come, she said, because "the idea of exploring other personas, male or female, is exciting, and certainly it's more fun and courageous to play with gender than to leave it alone."

Tracy saw the course as a vehicle for "certain traits that I think I might be able to develop further if I were a man—mainly through the avenues of music and sports."

Peggy, a dancer, said she regarded the workshop as one possible means of eliminating sexism, the thoughtless everyday forms of repression against men and women alike. "I feel like I have to learn how to be an ally to men," she explained, "and this is a way for me to get some information firsthand about what it's like to be a man."

This prompted several members of the group to wonder "how many guys are dressing up as women in order to understand *us* better."

Tracy had based her character, a Stephen Sprouse look-alike called

Claudio, on someone she knew. "Not well," she hastened to add. "I've seen him around, and he's had a strong effect on me. He's seventeen, a musician—sort of a romantic figure, and I want to be him so I can feel what it's like. Men are heartthrobs in a way that women aren't— teenage girls just go nuts over this guy—and I want to get a lot closer to that experience than I'm able to as a woman. Because even women who know they have sex appeal, they don't feel like they own it the way men do. Whereas with guys, it belongs to them—it's theirs. I want to be able to take things like that for granted." Tracy hoped that becoming Claudio might bring her closer to the guy on which he was based, she said. Did he know that she was doing this? She looked horrified. "Absolutely not!"

As men, the group was no less motley than it had been before, when its members were women. One remarked that only an AA meeting could bring together in one room such a preposterous assortment of types.

Paula the reporter had reconceived herself as a professor in the English department at NYU, complaining, "I got stuck with a lot of freshman comp courses last semester." The effect she was going for was "a portly Robert Reich," she announced. "You know, that cute Jewish intellectual look." Being only five feet one and a half, she worried that she might lack authority as a man, so she chose to bulk out by going to a costume company and renting a paunch, sewn into an undershirt. Her name, she said, was David.

Caroline had become a hippie. Her long hair parted in the middle, she wore hiphugger jeans, a plaid shirt, a leather vest, and a suede thong around her neck. "I look at you," Raul—formerly Paula the dancer—told her, "and I think, Yeah, I'd be friends with him."

Anne introduced herself as Micky, an Irish lower-middle-class guy from New Jersey who worked in an electronics shop. By sheer coincidence, Roberto—née Ella—worked in an electronics shop, too, on Forty-second Street. Roberto had been born in Rio de Janeiro, but now he lived in Brooklyn.

Dana had started out dressed as her boyfriend but then changed her mind and became Daniel instead—a surfer from Cocoa Beach, Florida, a recent high-school graduate who drove a souped-up, low-to-the-ground car (a Chevy, he said) and hung out at the A&P.

The photographer for *The Washington Post*, the only bona fide guy in the room, shook his head. "This is getting to be confusing," he said to no one in particular.

I was now James, a self-styled downtown kind of guy, in an Armani suit on loan from a friend and a dark silk shirt buttoned at the collar; no tie. Originally from a suburb of Cleveland, he worked as a producer for a record company. Claudio, who played back-up guitar, hoped that James would come and hear his band at a bar in Jersey next weekend. James shrugged. He got requests like this all the time.

Peggy, the choreographer, was now a writer named Tom—"as gay as the day is long," she said.

Warily, the men studied themselves in the mirror, as if they might insult one another, or fly off the handle, or turn violent. There was no telling what they might do.

"No smiling," Diane reprimanded. "Because women smile constantly—it's really hard for us to get out of the habit. But smiling all the time is conceding territory: I'm friendly, I mean no harm. Remember, you want to be as opaque as possible. Formidable, even. The basis of masculinity is a bluff, a complete bluff. I got a lot of material watching George Bush on TV during Operation Desert Storm—there was no way you could read any kind of human expression in his body."

"Oh, my God," Maureen exclaimed, "I look like my ex-husband!" She stared at herself, transfixed. The other members of the class had been telling her that as a man, she looked gay. "I don't *think* my ex-husband is gay," she said. "Although I don't know what he's doing now."

My fears were more or less allayed at the sight of myself as a preposterously effeminate guy. Being a Ronald Colman look-alike, I decided, did not in and of itself disqualify me from that vast subset of humanity widely represented by supermodels, Sharon Stone, and Uma Thurman. My friend, however, regarded herself with a certain amount of consternation: everyone agreed that if they saw her on the street looking like this, they would take her for a man.

An ad hoc poll named Paula the dancer and Peggy, hands down, the most convincing. "It's amazing what a little five-o'clock shadow will do," Tracy marveled.

Direct address was proving to be a bit of a problem, since no sooner had the students learned one set of (women's) names than they now

PLATE 69

PLATE 70

PLATE 71

PLATE 72

PLATE 73

PLATE 74

PLATE 75

PLATE 76

PLATE 77

PLATE 78

PLATE 79

had to learn another. But this was all right, it was eventually agreed, since most men never seem to remember anybody's name anyway.

I remarked on how awkward it was "to move around with something pressing against your leg all the time."

"They say," Char, now a biker wearing a do-rag, contended, "that if you close your hand and mark the spot where your middle finger hits, then open it, that that's the length—from that spot to the tip of your finger—that your penis is erect." She closed her hand and opened it again. "Perfectly respectable," she concluded.

"I've checked it many times," Paula the dancer concurred, "and it's completely accurate."

Johnny begged to differ: "The guy I live with has a huge penis, and I'm sure his hand isn't that big."

"I have a long hand," Maureen observed. "It's much bigger than the penis I brought."

Marianne emitted a series of little coughs, choking on stray mustache hairs like a cat with a furball caught in its throat.

"What about the diameter?" Char asked.

"There's no telling," Paula the dancer replied. "I've never heard of any way to predict that."

The photographer from the *Post* corralled the subjects for the "after" picture. This time, they shoved their hands in their pockets and stared at the camera, defiant.

Diane had turned into an avid NRA member from Wilkes-Barre, Pennsylvania: Jurgen, of German descent, was a father of four, the manager of a local department store, wearing a dark shirt, slacks that fit tight through the hips, and suspenders patterned with deer. He was vehemently pro-life, not that anyone asked.

It was time to get down to business. Now the real work of being a man could begin. "We have almost all gay men this evening," Diane noted parenthetically, surveying the room. And then she launched into the introductory-level material—lessons in sitting, standing, walking.

"Women sit on the edges of seats," she said. "On the subway, they squeeze their knees together so as not to touch the thighs of the men sitting next to them. Men sit with their feet planted firmly on the ground, ready for action. You can see that they own the space. It all comes down to feeling that you deserve a place in the world, that you don't need anybody's approval or permission, that you're responsible for your own protection—that there's nothing beyond your control." The students sat with their legs apart, their hands on their knees, as if, after a lifetime of propriety, someone had finally told them that they could relax. This part was easy.

"Hands in a semi-clenched position," Diane instructed. "You can fold your arms, or put them behind your back. Posture's not as important to men as it is to women. You can round your shoulders, let your beer belly hang out—it will add to the authenticity of your character." Diane watched as the would-be men awkwardly arranged their limbs, squaring their stances, redistributing their weight from hips to shoulders. "The characters I invent for myself are men who represent an essentialist idea of masculinity, so that you can see the extreme," she explained. "But you guys are gay, so you may want to modify all this."

Having mastered standing, the class moved on to walking. "I want you to walk as if there were a moat around you," Diane said, "as if the boundaries of your space extend beyond your body in all directions. Have you ever noticed that men on the street just keep on walking in a straight line, and it's the women who get out of the way?" We nodded. Under Diane's tutorial eye, we lurched around the living area, trying out lumbering strides, looking like first-time sailors who hadn't found their sea legs. "The kind of man that I am," Diane said, by way of example, "walks from the shoulders, from side to side, and the rest of the body follows—like you're barging into the space."

"Diane," Marianne interrupted, "a little piece of your mustache just blew off."

Diane ignored this remark, taking it like a man. "Let's say somebody calls your name," she continued. "A woman would turn from the waist and look back over her shoulder. A man walks around in a circle until he's face-to-face with the person who called him: 'You talking to me? You'd better have something to say.' Again," she reminded us, "this is from the essentialist perspective."

And then the class sat down to dinner. Diane showed us how to pick up a styrofoam cup with the whole hand, and how to set it down again firmly. "Everything is done with a sense of purpose," she advised us. "Nothing is thrown away—nothing extraneous, nothing unnecessary."

"Do you think this bib is too femme?" Char asked. She had tucked her napkin into the neckline of her T-shirt.

"Eating is done very purposefully," Diane explained. "Follow the shortest possible route between the plate and your mouth. You don't want to be dainty about this. Elbows on the table. If you're drinking something, just toss it into your mouth."

Caroline remarked, tentatively, that this seemed a rather superficial way to go about becoming a man. Men, after all, were so much more than the sum total of their appearance and their gestures. The resulting silence implied her classmates' agreement, though no one spoke up, for fear, perhaps, of offending the professor. "But then," Caroline continued, "you think of what happens when men dress as women, and that's a totally superficial view of who *we* are."

Someone wondered aloud whether superficiality was a notion that would even come up for discussion in a roomful of men imitating women—not because men are superficial by nature but because so much of femininity resides on the surface, whereas masculinity (presumably) emanates from within, as the outward evidence of a man's integrity and strength of character.

Peggy watched Maureen drinking soda. The hand position was correct: fingers close together, as if encased in a mitten; the grip a little tighter than necessary, advertising an excess of strength. But she seemed to be *sipping*—a giveaway. She looked to Peggy for an appraisal. "A little Mister Rogers," Peggy said, somewhat reluctantly.

"Oh, no," Maureen replied, crestfallen.

"Would you please pass the butter?" Paula asked.

"Oh, sorry," Tracy replied.

"Now that's the kind of thing a woman would say," Diane remarked. "She apologizes because she's been monopolizing the butter, or because she didn't telepathically anticipate someone else's need for it."

"I've already spilled on my tie," Marianne declared, staring at the spot.

Diane watched Tracy munch on a sprig of Italian parsley. "Men always leave the garnish," she said.

"Tom," Johnny said, "your mustache is coming off on the side—let me fix it. Tom?"

Paula the dancer tapped Peggy on the shoulder. "That's you."

Over dessert, the conversation turned to previous drag experience. Tracy recalled that once, dressed as Mariel Hemingway's husband— i.e., the killer—in *Star 80*, she went out with a woman friend who was also in drag, and they sat at a bar talking about other women, about their breasts and butts. "I didn't know I was going to turn into that kind of animal," she said. "I think drag makes me look at women differently—it makes me feel like I'm capable of objectifying and possessing them."

Anne had gone out as a man with other women friends in drag. They spent the evening in a bar. "The weird thing," she said, "was the way women would relate to us. We made them anxious. I wasn't used to threatening women."

In an exercise reminiscent of beginning drama workshops, the students took turns improvising conversations, interacting with one another as men. There were certain lapses, which the vigilant audience was quick to point out: the extensive curiosity about family life, which struck most members of the class as a particularly feminine line of questioning; a telltale gesture, like tucking a stray wisp of hair behind one's ear. "A man would push his hair back with his whole hand," Diane interjected. "When a man touches his face, it's with the back of his hand or with his thumb but not with his fingertips. As women," she added, "we're so observant of male behavior that all the stuff I'm showing you, you already know inherently."

Jane Austen is reported to have said that she didn't write scenes between men because she didn't know what men talked about when they were alone together. Neither, evidently, did we. We often found ourselves at a loss for words in our impromptu exchanges.

Late afternoon. A cluttered studio apartment, dominated by a set of drums and an upright piano. Miles peruses Claudio's collection of CD's. Claudio sits on the edge of the bed, which is unmade, mindlessly strumming chords on an acoustic guitar.

MILES: How's that love song you were working on? Was it Shirley?

CLAUDIO: Marsha.

MILES: Marsha, right.

CLAUDIO: Yeah, she was hot. I liked working on the music, but she wanted to be with me all the time, and I just couldn't handle it.

Rush hour. A busy street in midtown Manhattan. Rounding the corner, Bob runs into Andy, whom he hasn't seen in over two years.

BOB: How ya doin'? [He shoves his hands in his pockets.]

ANDY: Pretty good, pretty good. Business as usual. [He tugs at the pocket flaps on his jacket.] How's it at home?

BOB: I don't think it's going to work out.

ANDY: Too bad. [He shakes his head.] Well, life goes on.

Interior of a subway car on the Seventh Avenue IRT.

TOM: How're things at home?

RAUL: Fuck home. I don't want to talk about home.

Midnight. A deserted parking lot on a back street in Hoboken. Micky and Roberto circle each other.

ROBERTO: What about that money?

MICKY: What money?

ROBERTO: Is there a problem here?

Early evening. Cocktail hour at the Wilkes-Barre Ramada Inn. A piano playing in the background. The class of '65 gathers for its twenty-fifth high-school reunion.

DAVID: Jurgen, how are you? Good to see you!

JURGEN: Oh, I lost my wife.

DAVID: Tough when that happens.

JURGEN: Well, I'll get another one.

"When you actually become a man," Diane said, "you realize that so much of it is a big lie. And we go through life pretending that they're superior to us."

Then she turned on a tape, and the guys danced. To the convivial reggae strains of "Iko, Iko," we jived, twisting from side to side, our movements falling, woodenly, slightly to the right or the left of the downbeat. Diane advised the class that the most crucial aspect of dancing as a man was controlling the hip movement (Mick Jagger and Elvis being the exceptions, not the rule). Pelvises still. The students gyrated intently, from the waist up, as if dancing required great powers of concentration—each in his own airtight bubble, in a limited range, feet nailed to the floor. For a brief moment, the living area took on the forlorn aspect of a club populated by the kind of guys whom the women taking part in Torr's workshop would have pegged as losers. In friendship and in love, these women aspired to a new breed of man, and, every so often, they could imagine him; in their minds, they'd pieced together a sort of collective portrait. Mostly, what he would be had been arrived at by way of what he *wouldn't* be—that much, at least, was clear. Still, when the time came to dress in drag, they didn't dare become him. Cozy, affectionate, communicative, he inspired in them feelings of solidarity that real men—the men they knew—rarely, if ever, inspired. His fears were theirs for the moment: What if, in the harsh light of day, he didn't pass muster? What if he weren't man enough? It would be just a matter of time before the world was on to the fact that this was not a man but an imposter and an unsuccessful one, at that. And then, despite the stubble on his chin and the gruff gestures and the suit that emphasized the breadth of his shoulders, the jig would be up. Masculinity, no less than femininity, is an undertaking, and those who are unsuccessful in their efforts—all the failed men—are branded women.

ANXIETY

The apparent individual conflict of the patient is revealed as a universal conflict of his environment and epoch. Neurosis is thus nothing less than an individual attempt, however unsuccessful, to solve a universal problem.

C. G. JUNG,
New Paths in Psychology

....

Postmodernist thinkers, who contend that gender is a cultural construct, could ask for no better mascot than a drag queen. The discourse may be esoteric: try out the ideas of Robert Stoller, say, or Judith P. Butler on the businessmen riding the bullet train in Tokyo, or on the regular clients at a café in Berlin, or on the baseball fans at Yankee Stadium, and chances are that the response will be bewilderment. But drag puts the abstract into practice, illustrating one of the theory's central tenets. Looking at a drag queen, we instantly grasp the distinction between male (a biological category) and masculine (a cultural category), between female and feminine; they are obviously not one and the same.

In the wake of recent attempts to overhaul our criteria for masculinity and femininity, we have been forced to examine our own and one another's behavior to such an extent that we have come to recognize it for the pose that it is. Postmodernism sees through that pose and at the same time legitimizes it. Each and every one of us is a walking catalogue of allusions to the movies we've seen, the stories we've taken to heart, the people we've known; we appropriate an actor's gesture, a character's fate, a friend's expression. In the aggre-

162 gate of these little impersonations and the mutations we bring to them lies our identity.

By exaggerating the performance, by taking it all the way to the brink of the ridiculous, drag calls everybody's bluff: biker types in black leather, bleached blondes in low-cut dresses, gay men in muscle T-shirts and construction boots, wide-eyed waifs in long, flowing gowns are all thrown into stark relief. As Anne Hollander has said, "Clothes create selves, rather than sitting on top of them." In a process not all that different from a drag queen's, a woman selects an archetype consistent with her aspirations and her potential—the Siren, perhaps, or the Ingenue, the Gamine, the Tough Cookie—and then crafts her own interpretation on the basis of the examples available to her. There is no original to be copied, Judith P. Butler contends; there are only "imitative practices which refer laterally to other imitations." So women imitate one another, drag queens imitate women, and—lately—women may imitate drag queens.

Along with the liberty inherent in the notion that we are all actors—playing women, playing men—comes a certain queasiness brought on by the realization that nothing in our understanding of the roles we play is absolute or fixed. For many people, it has proved all too tempting to lay the blame for the current turmoil at the feminists' doorstep—as if the crisis in sex roles had been brought on overnight by a few embittered troublemakers, as if the fragile equilibrium that existed before women came into their own were preferable to this free-for-all. And it's true: the old order offered a certitude that is conspicuously missing from the postmodern era. Even feminism itself can no longer muster a consensus, having fallen into disarray and splintered into factions. Wendy Kaminer proposes that "equal-rights feminism" was doomed for a number of reasons, among them the fact that "it challenged men and women to shape their own identities without resort to stereotypes."

Drag revives those stereotypes and mocks them at the same time. No matter how elastic our criteria for masculinity and femininity, drag flouts them. It relies for its impact on our stubborn conviction that the two sexes, equal or not, are in any case opposite—a model that polarizes men and women. More worrisome than any threat that drag queens seem to pose are the intimations of chaos that pervade our daily lives, a chaos that drag queens keep at bay, if only for the time

being. Drag is, ultimately, political, with a subtext that is easily lost
amid the feather boas, the false eyelashes, the florid gestures. To the
extent that its fascination has largely resided in seeing members of the
ruling class assume the guise of the ruled, drag has been strikingly
similar to blackface. Like blacks, women have historically constituted
an underclass. Like blackface, drag has articulated a widespread nostalgia for a time when the oppressed were seemingly happy with their
lot. Those were the days, before the unrest and the animosity set in, before the list of demands was drawn up.

In blackface or in drag, men have adopted, temporarily, the style
and mannerisms of a "minority" population. This has been their prerogative, a kind of *droit de seigneur* that they could exercise with im-
punity, becoming black or a woman for the sake of amusement, on a
whim. Disconcerting as the sight of a man in a dress may have been,
it was never the grab for power that a woman in a man's clothes used
to be, before women acquired many of the rights that belonged exclusively to men; no black entertainers worked in whiteface. Manhood—
white manhood in particular—was ordained by God, and it could not
be approximated. Like blackface performers, many drag queens
stopped short of head-to-toe verisimilitude. Chest hair, big biceps left
exposed, falsies that look implausible, a wig slightly askew, or simply
a prominent Adam's apple—*something* belied the feminine appearance and announced: "This is a *convention.*" Beneath the trappings
was a man, still in control.

Both blackface and drag are lexicons of mannerisms.

Like Al Jolson and other entertainers who specialized in "Negro"
numbers, men in drag have caricatured the means by which those
who are not in power ingratiate themselves to those who are. Blackface came into its own on the vaudeville stage and in early movies, but
the drag renaissance that is currently under way is as much social as
it is theatrical: its practitioners appear not only on the stage but at
bars and parties, taking its message into the streets. But the message
is not the same as it used to be. The basis of our fascination with the
sight of a man in drag has changed.

Recent developments in psychology suggest an alternative reason
why we find a man who dresses as a woman intriguing and provocative. Freud's model of masculinity as the dominant sex, with girls
forced to deviate from it, has given way to a new understanding,

which holds that boys and girls alike identify with their mothers initially, and that it is the boys who must eventually differentiate themselves. Contrary to what Freud proposed, then, it is the feminine that is, briefly, universal, and the masculine that is formulated in response to it. Our mutually exclusive definitions of the sexes are traceable to that moment when a boy must become the antithesis of his mother.

A woman today may move freely across the entire range of possible traits: she may be strong or weak, aggressive or passive, beautiful or brainy, or both; she may wear a skirt or pants, high heels or flats; she may crop her hair short or leave it long and loose; she may pursue any number of interests, from a career in the military to ballet lessons, from the law to interior decoration. No matter what she does, she will still be a woman; very little in the way of her behavior or appearance can jeopardize her femininity.

Forays across the border into the other sex's territory prove to be far more perilous for men than they are for women. Much of human experience is effectively off-limits to a man: he must not be timid, or soft, or emotional. Any preoccupation with esthetic matters or domestic pursuits runs the risk of compromising his masculinity. Being labeled a "sissy" is far worse than being labeled a "tomboy"; "boyish," applied to a woman, may be a compliment in some instances, but "effeminate," applied to a man, never is.

When women's campaign for equal rights finally succeeded in opening the door to sports, politics, and any number of other fields that had previously been closed to them, men were expected to embrace cooking and fashion en masse; the "Peacock Revolution" was gleefully hailed as their introduction to the joys of dressing up. As it turned out, the revolution was short-lived. Given the opportunity to explore what has traditionally been considered feminine, the majority of men—drag queens excepted—have done so reluctantly and hardly at all, for the (now) obvious reason that it is simply too dangerous. A man, it seems, is only a man to the extent that he is not a woman.

If "feminism represents, in the popular view, a rejection of femininity," as Wendy Kaminer has suggested, then drag queens have stepped into the void that feminism created. With each sex defined in relation to the other, the end of femininity would spell the demise of masculinity as well. Being a woman is a tough job, but somebody's got to do it, perpetuating a femininity that, to the minds of most drag queens, is severely endangered if not already extinct.

The songs are always the same: in drag bars, in dance clubs, in Bangkok, New York, or Berlin, the bass throbs with the urgency of a heart about to burst as Shirley Bassey or Gloria Gaynor or Debbie Gibson announces the loss of love in a keening melody, and a chorus of male voices sings along, an octave lower. "I, who have nothing . . ." "I will survive . . ." "I know I'll never love that way again . . ." These are the drag anthems. They represent a consensus that the real Marlene Dietrich and the real Naomi Campbell could never reach. On the downbeat, men dressed as women with little or nothing in common are united in their longing for a vanished femininity: full-time, all-consuming, self-sacrificing, torch-carrying. The singer—a woman who built her life around a man, dressing for his approval, catering to his whims—has been disappointed, and an ersatz sorority, convened for an evening, commiserates. Yes, they concur, a man's love is everything; they strive for it, they cling to it, and when it is withdrawn, they resolve to carry on with an effort that is nothing short of heroic.

Paradoxically, the image of a drag queen teetering in high heels now presents itself as a surprisingly apt metaphor for the precariousness of masculinity.

Drag plays on our eagerness to suspend disbelief, on our desire to see a woman where there is none: the woman is in the eye of the beholder. The message is sent in shorthand, by means of traits apparent at first glance. (For the purposes of imitation, particularly of imitating someone famous, as few as three signals may suffice, e.g., Carmen Miranda: sarong, turban, fruit.) Jean Baudrillard calls this the "transsubstantiation of sex into signs" and claims it is "the secret of all seduction."

Fetishism, as a peculiarly male phenomenon, has been attributed to the ownership of a penis, of a body part on which all sexual attention is focused. Men may look at women with a fetishistic eye, but women do not reciprocate; when Freud divided the world into the haves and the have-nots, this much turned out to be true. The penis, idealized, becomes the phallus, inspiring an endless number of highly personal myths. Drag queens who work as hookers report that their customers are straight and consequently susceptible to the signals of a woman, regardless of whether those signals are being sent by a woman.

By triggering reactions that are entirely reflexive, drag upholds the very definitions that it subverts; it is at once radical and deeply conventional. To the extent that it is also misogynistic, one of its most pernicious aspects is surely its uncanny knack for depersonalizing women, for reducing them time and again to a semaphore: hair, lips, breasts, hips, high heels. Recent attempts to portray women in all their complexity, to rise above this tendency to see them as objects, come to grief in drag. The force of fetishism overrides all good intentions, even common sense. So it happens that the man who buys into the usual signals may find himself the victim of a scam. Those who rail against drag for the ways in which it satirizes women seem to overlook the far more subtle and invidious ways in which it humiliates men.

Drag is a man's initiation into the cult of beauty. The hair salon, the fashion magazine, the slumber party have been the secret precincts of a sisterhood founded on ancient lore and privileged information, and fostered by homosexuals, like eunuchs in the harem. Women have come together to ready themselves for men, trading tips and products, with a billion-dollar industry to support their efforts.

While most women grudgingly tolerate the hard work that femininity requires—submitting to manicures and fittings and facials, undergoing waxing and electrolysis, standing in shoes that pinch their feet—drag queens often embrace it, regarding the bother and the pain with a certain exalted romanticism. Putting on makeup, they mimic the expressions that a woman makes when she is alone with her reflection, playing to no one but herself: the haughtiness with which she tilts her head back and looks down her nose as she applies her eyeliner; the way she watches, sidelong, as she brushes color on her cheekbones; the slackjawed concentration with which she puts on lipstick and then, in a businesslike grimace, presses her lips together to blot it.

Like drag queens, women rely on illusion. In the interest of illusion, they exaggerate certain features and downplay others. These tactics, which drag employs, are by no means mysterious: women make use of them all the time, and to such foolproof effect that we rarely, if ever, question a woman's rendering of her own features. Her interpretation becomes her face in our minds. The image supersedes the reality and distorts it.

We proceed on our assumptions. If A equals B, then B equals A: if women wear red lipstick, then someone wearing red lipstick must be a woman. Drag lays bare the fallacy in our logic, and demonstrates the extent to which the feminine ideal has become anonymous and abstract, divorced from what women really look like.

Just as drag queens parody women, turning them into a cartoon, women parody themselves when it suits them. It is said that Marilyn Monroe could go unrecognized on the street in New York because she wasn't doing what she herself called "the walk." Drag highlights the ironic distance between the pretense and the person, male or female, underneath—a distance with which many women are already familiar. When, in 1973, the Hasty Pudding Club changed its "Woman of the Year" award to the (one time only) "Person of the Year" and bestowed it on Gloria Steinem, she remarked, "I don't mind drag— women have been female impersonators for some time." It was John Waters who coined the term "female female impersonators" to describe women overtly simulating femininity.

For the sake of female beauty, "kings have been dethroned and dynasties perished," a turn-of-the-century advertisement for face cream proclaimed. Writers of the period tended to dwell on Delilah, Cleopatra, the Queen of Sheba, Madame de Pompadour, the Empress Josephine, and other legendary ravishing women whose looks subjugated the conquerors of empires. Given women's lives at the time and their limited prospects, this hyperbole seems intended to reassure women that they had not gotten a raw deal—that, as the repositories of men's fantasies, they could rule the world.

Since then, the influence that beauty wields has grown enormously, thanks to the progress of photography and the proliferation of the media. In magazines and newspapers, on television, the image holds sway, commanding our attention and beguiling our imaginations. The distant promise extended to women at the start of the century by journalists and cosmetics manufacturers—the promise that beauty triumphs over achievement—has been fulfilled in ways they could never have imagined, in the global celebrity of women like Madonna and Princess Diana.

Today, men in drag are every bit as threatening as women in drag used to be, and for the same reason: they represent a bid for power that has been denied them—in this case, the power of beauty. While women have made significant inroads into the realm of ideas, they have also retained control of the realm of appearances, and all the audacity, the simmering envy, the frustration and resentment that was once implicit in women's dressing as men are now echoed in men's dressing as women. In our relentlessly visual culture, what Jean Baudrillard calls "the immense privilege of the feminine"—the privilege of not being accountable to truth or meaning or content, of dwelling entirely on the surface—now reigns supreme and reaches its zenith in the careers of supermodels, whose voices are never heard, though their faces are ubiquitous.

Implicit in much, if not most, of drag's current manifestations is a defection, however temporary, from the ranks of men. The conviction that women are better or, at the very least, that women *have it* better is seemingly rampant. Women have more fun; they have more freedom. Their visual currency, which one hundred years ago amounted to little more than a consolation prize, has dramatically risen in value in a culture that has become increasingly visual. When a man does drag today, he puts on the trappings of women's power, and the naked exhilaration that ensues is so palpable, it's contagious. We are living in a hall of mirrors. In drag, we witness the triumph of illusion.

PLATES

46 Zaldy and Mathú, Wigstock, New York City, 1991

47 Lavinia Co-op

48 Butch Chanel: John, Robert, and Michael

49 Zaldy, Kylie, and Mathú

50 Tabboo!

51 Ebony Jet

52 RuPaul

53 Kabuki Starshine

54 Miss Guy

55 LaHoma Van Zandt

56 Alexander

57 Ulrich Suss

58 Ming Vauze

59 Constance

60 John Kelly as Joni Mitchell (Plates 47–60: all photographs, Wigstock, New York City, 1992)

61 John Kelly as Barbette, "A Strange Beauty," New York City, 1992

62 Mike, studio, New York City, 1991

63 Trash, studio, New York City, 1991

64 Cristina Grajales, New York City, 1992 (stylist, Kathy Levin)

65 Amanda LePore as Jayne Mansfield in *The Girl Can't Help It*, studio, New York City, 1995

66 J. Alexander, Paris, 1992 (makeup, Earnest)

67 Simon Doonan, at home, New York City, 1992

68 Her Imperial Highness, the Grand Duchess Regina Fong, Last of the Romanoffs [sic], Kensington, London, 1991

69 Wig, Wigstock, New York City, 1991

70 Imperial Court of New York, New York City, 1993

71 Delilah, Empress 17 of the Silver Dollar Court, Reno, Nevada 1993

72 Sheila Tequila, studio, London, 1992

73 Dixie, at home, New York City, 1992

74 The Invasion of the Pines, Fire Island, New York, July 1992

75 Hattie Hathaway, Housing Works Benefit, New York, 1993

76 New York City, 1992

77 London, 1992

78 Finalists in the Femme Queen Face category work it for the judges at the House of Omni Ball, New York City, 1994

79 Mike, East Hampton, New York, 1991

front cover: Legs, studio, New York City, 1991
back cover: Mike, East Hampton, New York, 1991

ACKNOWLEDGMENTS

Before listing the strangers, acquaintances, and friends whose generosity has enabled me to write this book, I want to extend my sincere apologies to those I have omitted. In the course of my travels, I encountered so many people who gave of their time, their ideas, and their insights that I have come to think of this book as the aggregate of their contributions, and to the extent that this roster is incomplete, I regret the omissions.

I am particularly grateful to the following people:

In Rio de Janeiro: Jared Braiterman, for his time and insight; Deborah Cohen, Marissa Alvarez Lima, and Guilherme Araujo, for their suggestions; Alberto Pinheiro, for his time and cooperation.

In Paris: Lola, Blanca Li and Etienne, Jay Alexander, Damien, Michel Cressol, and Alberto Sorbelli, for their time, their ideas, and the benefit of their experience; Ina Delcourt, David Seidner, Hélie Lassaigne, for perspective.

In Tokyo: Emi Murakami and the Diamonds Are Forever crew, for their good-natured participation; Donald Richie and Henry Scott Stokes, for their wisdom; Yasumasa Morimura, for his cooperation, and Yoshiko Isshiki and the Luhring-Augustine Gallery (in New York), for their assistance; Issey Miyake, Nancy Knox and Jun Kanai, Jan Kawata, Masako Kitagami, and Patrick Smith, for intercession and guidance; Kako Seike, Takako Mishina, and Toshihiro Kuno, for their skills in translation.

In Berlin: Freo Gunther Majer, for research and translations; Charlotte von Mahlsdorf, for her candor; Matthias Frings, Bev Stroganov, Ichgola Androgyn, Ovomaltine, Tima die Gottliche, Martin Ostrowsky, Strapsharry, Kaspar Kameleon, for their time and observations; Dorothea von Moltke (in New York), for translations.

In Amsterdam: Frans Kubin, Franck Wydebos, and Emile, for their time and insight; Frans Ankone, for his hospitality, his friendship, and translation.

In London: Gerlinda Costiff, Andrew Logan, Sheila Tequila, Hamish Bowles, and Guillermo Cabrera Infante, for their time and intelligence.

In Bangkok: Luke Hardy and Michael Biersdorfer, for their generosity, their understanding, their skills in translation, and their companionship.

In New York: Diane Torr and my fellow classmates in her Drag Kings Workshop, for their candor and their trust; Susanne Bartsch, for her irrepressible curiosity, her companionship, and her unstinting help; Baroness,

174   Louis Canales, Alan Mace, Larry Ree, Gina Germaine, Mathú Andersen and Zaldy, and Marc Jacobs, for their time and cooperation; Kevin Ultra Omni, Lee's Mardi Gras (Lee, Bubbles, Dixie, Terry), and the organizers of the invasion of the Pines (Pansy, in particular), for their hospitality; Kal Ruttenstein, Rob Wynne and Charles Ruas, Robert Woolley, Simon Doonan, Elliott Jurist, and Lois Feinblatt, for reconnaissance.

And in general: Adam Walsh and Manuel Sanches, for their meticulous transcriptions, with marginalia that were often funny and thought-provoking; Judith Thurman, Gini Alhadeff, Judy Kinberg, Bob Gottlieb, and Guy Trebay, for moral support and invaluable editorial suggestions; Romeo Gigli, for his generosity and companionship; Sam Perkins, for his kindness in filling in the blanks.

And, finally, the relay team of editors: Susan Kamil and Joni Evans, whose enthusiasm got the ball rolling; Helen Morris, who kept it in motion; and Deb Futter, who took it and ran with it. Jeanne Pinault, who expunged the excess dashes and otherwise groomed my copy. Sarah Chalfant and Andrew Wylie, whose patience and faith have seen me through.

And, last, a thousand thanks to Michael O'Brien, for having the idea in the first place and for capturing in images the spirit of what I wanted to say.

HOLLY BRUBACH

This book is dedicated to Robert McElroy and Zoltan Gerliczki.

Special thanks to Holly Brubach; our terrific editor, Deb Futter; my agent, Amanda Urban; Rochelle Udell; Susan Kamil; Susanne Bartsch; my photo assistants Julian Imrie, Cory Dunham, and Natalia Baca; Tre Temperilli; Matthew Barney; Chi Chi Valenti; Johnny Dynell and everyone at Jackie 60; Robbin Schiff for our great cover; Hattie Hathaway; John Kelly; Evelyn Dallal; Elisabeth Novick; Empress Windswept Domination; William Wilson; Nicola Kotsoni; Debbie Keith and Louis Gisone for all the beautiful black-and-white printing.

And in memorium: Mike Gonzales, Anthony Wong, and Dorian Corey.

MICHAEL JAMES O'BRIEN

178 Reynolds, Simon, and Joy Press. *The Sex Revolts: Gender, Rebellion and Rock 'n' Roll.* Cambridge, Mass.: Harvard University Press, 1995.

Rhode, Deborah L., ed. *Theoretical Perspectives on Sexual Difference.* New Haven and London: Yale University Press, 1990.

Saikaku, Ihara. *The Great Mirror of Male Love.* (English translation by Paul Gordon Schalow. Stanford: Stanford University Press, 1990.)

Sarduy, Severo. *Written on a Body.* (English translation by Carol Maier. New York: Lumen Books, 1989.)

Selby, Hubert, Jr. *Last Exit to Brooklyn.* New York: Grove Press, 1964.

Sievers, Sharon L. *Flowers in Salt: The Beginnings of Feminist Consciousness in Modern Japan.* Stanford: Stanford University Press, 1983.

Stoller, Robert J., M.D. *Presentations of Gender.* New Haven: Yale University Press, 1985.

———. *Sex and Gender: The Development of Masculinity and Femininity.* London: Karnac Books reprint, 1984; copyright, 1968.

Sullivan, Louis. *From Female to Male: The Life of Jack Bee Garland.* Boston: Alyson Publications, 1990.

Thompson, Keith, ed. *To Be a Man: In Search of the Deep Masculine.* Los Angeles: Jeremy P. Tarcher, 1991.

Winford, E. Carlton. *Femme Mimics: A Pictorial Record of Female Impersonators.* Dallas: Winford Company, 1954.

Woodhouse, Annie. *Fantastic Women: Sex, Gender and Transvestism.* New Brunswick, N.J.: Rutgers University Press, 1989.

Woolf, Virginia. *Orlando.* New York: Harcourt, Brace and Company, 1928.

Core, Philip. *Camp: The Lie That Tells the Truth*. New York: Delilah, 1984.

Cossey, Caroline. *My Story*. London: Faber and Faber, 1991.

Crisp, Quentin. *The Naked Civil Servant*. New York: Holt, Rinehart and Winston, 1968.

Cunningham, Michael. *Flesh and Blood*. New York: Farrar Straus and Giroux, 1995.

Dalby, Liza. *Kimono: Fashioning Culture*. New Haven and London: Yale University Press, 1993.

Dekker, Rudolf M., and Lotte C. van de Pol. *The Tradition of Female Transvestism in Early Modern Europe*. Foreward by Peter Burke. London: Macmillan Press, 1989.

Docter, Richard F. *Transvestites and Transsexuals: Toward a Theory of Cross-Gender Behavior*. New York: Plenum Press, 1988.

Easthope, Antony. *What a Man's Gotta Do: The Masculine Myth in Popular Culture*. Boston: Unwin Hyman, 1990.

Ellis, Havelock. *Studies in the Psychology of Sex*. New York: Random House, 1942.

Epstein, Julia, and Kristina Straub, eds. *Body Guards: The Cultural Politics of Gender Ambiguity*. New York and London: Routledge, 1991.

Farrer, Peter, ed. *Men in Petticoats: A Selection of Letters from Victorian Newspapers*. Liverpool: Karn Publications Garston, 1987.

Fast, Irene. *Gender Identity: A Differentiation Model*. Hillsdale, N.J.: The Analytic Press, 1984.

Fischer, Gerhard. "Pierre Molinier," in *Camera Austria International*, No. 36.

Fuss, Diana. *Essentially Speaking: Feminism, Nature & Difference*. New York and London: Routledge, 1989.

Garber, Marjorie. *Vested Interests: Cross-Dressing & Cultural Anxiety*. New York: Routledge, 1991.

————, ed. *Media Spectacles*. New York: Routledge, 1993.

Gilmore, David D. *Manhood in the Making: Cultural Concepts of Masculinity*. New Haven and London: Yale University Press, 1990.

Hare-Mustin, Rachel T., and Jeanne Marecek, eds. *Making a Difference: Psychology and the Construction of Gender*. New Haven: Yale University Press, 1990.

Hirschfeld, Magnus, M.D. *Die Transvestiten*. (English translation by Michael A. Lombardi-Nash. *Transvestites: The Erotic Drive to Cross-Dress*. Buffalo, N.Y.: Prometheus Books, 1991.)

Hollander, Anne. *Sex and Suits*. New York: Alfred A. Knopf, 1994.

Homberg, Octave, and Fernand Jousselin, eds. *D'Éon de Beaumont: His Life*

and Times. (English translation by Alfred Rieu. London: Martin Secker, 1911.)

Hudson, Liam, and Bernadine Jacot. *The Way Men Think: Intellect, Intimacy and the Erotic Imagination.* New Haven and London: Yale University Press, 1991.

Kaminer, Wendy. "Feminism's Identity Crisis." *The Atlantic,* October 1993.

Kaplan, Louise J. *Female Perversions: The Temptations of Emma Bovary.* New York: Doubleday, 1991.

Kidwell, Claudia Brush, and Valerie Steele. *Men and Women: Dressing the Part.* Washington, D.C.: Smithsonian Institution Press, 1989.

Kondo, Dorinne K. *Crafting Selves: Power, Gender, and Discourses of Identity in a Japanese Workplace.* Chicago and London: University of Chicago Press, 1990.

Kroker, Arthur and Marilouise, eds. *The Hysterical Male: New Feminist Theory.* New York: St. Martin's Press, 1991.

The Lady Chablis, with Theodore Boulokos. *Hiding My Candy.* New York: Pocket Books, 1996.

Laqueur, Thomas. *Making Sex: Body and Gender from the Greeks to Freud.* Cambridge, Mass.: Harvard University Press, 1990.

Lesser, Wendy. *His Other Half: Men Looking at Women Through Art.* Cambridge, Mass.: Harvard University Press, 1991.

Lingis, Alphonso. *Abuses.* Berkeley: University of California Press, 1994.

Malaparte, Curzio. *La pelle.* Milan: Mondadori, 1978. (English translation by David Moore. *The Skin.* Marlboro, Vt.: The Marlboro Press, 1988.)

Mishima, Yukio. *Kinjiki.* Tokyo: Shinchosha, 1951. (English translation by Alfred H. Marks. *Forbidden Colors.* New York: Alfred A. Knopf, 1968.)

Morgan, Fidelis, with Charlotte Charke. *The Well-Known Troublemaker: A Life of Charlotte Charke.* London and Boston: Faber and Faber, 1988.

Newton, Esther. *Mother Camp: Female Impersonators in America.* Chicago and London: University of Chicago Press, 1972, 1979.

Odzer, Cleo. *Patpong Sisters: An American Woman's View of the Bangkok Sex World.* New York: Blue Moon Books/Arcade Publishing, 1994.

Olivier, Christiane. *Les Enfants de Jocaste: L'empreinte de la mère.* Paris: Éditions Denoël/Gonthier, 1980.

Paglia, Camille. *Sexual Personae: Art and Decadence from Nefertiti to Emily Dickinson.* New Haven: Yale University Press, 1990.

Penley, Constance, and Sharon Willis, eds. *Male Trouble.* Minneapolis: University of Minnesota Press, 1993.

Perchuk, Andrew, and Helaine Posner, eds. *The Masculine Masquerade: Masculinity and Repression.* Cambridge, Mass.: MIT Press, 1995.

A READING LIST

Ackroyd, Peter. *Dressing Up: Transvestism and Drag: The History of an Obsession.* New York: Simon and Schuster, 1979.

Allen, J. J. *The Man in the Red Velvet Dress: Inside the World of Cross-Dressing.* New York: Carol Publishing Group, 1996.

Badinter, Elisabeth. *L'Un est l'autre.* Paris: Éditions Odile Jacob, 1986. (English translation by Barbara Wright. *The Un-opposite Sex: The End of the Gender Battle.* New York: Harper & Row, 1989.)

Barthes, Roland. *L'Empire des signes.* Geneva: Skira, 1970. (English translation by Richard Howard. *Empire of Signs.* New York: Hill and Wang, 1982.)

Baudrillard, Jean. *Séduction.* Paris: Éditions Galilée, 1979. (English translation by Brian Singer. *Seduction.* New York: St. Martin's Press, 1990.)

Berendt, John. *Midnight in the Garden of Good and Evil.* New York: Random House, 1994.

Breen, Dana, ed. *The Gender Conundrum.* London: Routledge, 1983.

Brierley, Harry. *Transvestism: A Handbook with Case Studies for Psychologists, Psychiatrists and Counsellors.* New York: Pergamon Press, 1979.

Bulliet, C. J. *Venus Castina: Famous Female Impersonators Celestial and Human.* New York: Bonanza Books, 1928, 1956.

Burke, Phyllis. *Gender Shock: Exploding the Myths of Male and Female.* New York: Anchor Books, 1996.

Butler, Judith. *Gender Trouble: Feminism and the Subversion of Identity.* New York: Routledge, 1990.

————. *Bodies That Matter: On the Discursive Limits of "Sex."* New York: Routledge, 1993.

Chabon, Michael. *Wonder Boys.* New York: Villard Books, 1995.

Chapman, Rowena, and Jonathan Rutherford, eds. *Male Order: Unwrapping Masculinity.* London: Lawrence & Wishart, 1988.

Chermayeff, Catherine, Jonathan David, and Nan Richardson. *Drag Diaries.* San Francisco: Chronicle Books, 1995.

Choisy, l'Abbé de. *Mémoires.* Paris: Mercure de France, 1983.

Cocteau, Jean. *Le Numéro Barbette.* Photographs by Man Ray. Paris: Jacques Damase, 1980.

Colette. *Le Pur et l'impur.* (English translation by Herma Briffault. *The Pure and the Impure.* London: Secker and Warburg, 1968.)

ABOUT THE AUTHORS

HOLLY BRUBACH is the former style editor of *The New York Times Magazine.* She has also served as *The New Yorker*'s fashion columnist and as a staff writer for *The Atlantic.* Born in Pittsburgh, she lives in Milan and New York.

A photographer for nearly two decades, MICHAEL JAMES O'BRIEN studied at Yale with Walker Evans. His fashion and portrait work has been featured in *Newsweek, Rolling Stone, Donna, The New York Times,* and *Elle Decor.* Since 1993 he has produced still photography for artist Matthew Barney. He lives in New York City.

ABOUT THE TYPE

This book was set in Bodoni, a typeface designed by Giambattista Bodoni (1740–1813), the renowned Italian printer and type designer. Bodoni originally based his letter forms on those of the Frenchman Fournier, and created his type to have beautiful contrasts between light and dark.